THE
POWER
OF YOUR
DREAMS

D0172226

Yesterday
is but to-day's memory
and
To-morrow
is to-day's dream

(*Kahlil Gibran, the prophet*)

With all my love
for Inge, Rosemarie, Wilma, Hanjo, Frances, Yvonne,
Val, Kay, Desmond, and dreamers everywhere,
especially those whose dreams
have inspired this book

Heather Wachter.

THE
POWER
OF YOUR
DREAMS

Soozi Holbeche

PIATKUS

Acknowledgements

My love and a big thank you to Desmond, without whose love, support, encouragement and typing skills this book would never have reached completion. Thank you also to Gill who helped me over the hiccups and to Judy whose idea it was in the first place. Love and thanks to Paul Solomon who showed me that both dreams and life truly are the language of the gods.

© 1991 Soozi Holbeche

First published in Great Britain in 1991 by
Judy Piatkus (Publishers) Ltd of
5 Windmill Street, London W1P 1HF

First paperback edition 1992

The moral right of the author has been asserted

A *catalogue record for this book is available
from the British Library*

ISBN 0–7499–1051–8
0–7499–1151–4 (pbk)

Edited by Esther Jagger
Designed by Sue Ryall
Cover design by Jennie Smith

Set in Linotron Sabon by
Wyvern Typesetting Ltd, Bristol
Printed and bound in Great Britain by
Butler & Tanner Ltd, Frome and London

CONTENTS

	INTRODUCTION	7
	THE FIVE-POINTED STAR	10
1	DREAMS IN A TIME OF CHANGE	11
2	HOW DREAMS HELP US	28
3	THE LOST CHILD	40
4	SLEEP: AN ALTERED STATE OF CONSCIOUSNESS	50
5	THE GREAT DREAM INTERPRETERS	64
6	ETHNIC DREAMING TRADITIONS	77
7	DREAM INCUBATION	102
8	DIFFERENT KINDS OF DREAMS	113
9	DREAMS OF DEATH AND ASTRAL TRAVEL	130
10	HOW TO MAKE THE BEST USE OF YOUR DREAMS	144
11	SYMBOLS AND COLOURS IN DREAMS	172
	APPENDIX: DREAM GROUPS AND WORKSHOPS	182
	FURTHER READING	188
	USEFUL ADDRESSES	189
	INDEX	190

... We are in a time so strange
that living equals dreaming,
   and this teaches me that man
   dreams his life, awake.

The rich man dreams of fortune
   which causes him many worries;
      The poor man dreams of misery and misfortune,
the ambitious man dreams of ambition,
   the injured man dreams of vengeance;
      everyone in the world
         only dreams what he is
         without knowing it.

What is life? A lie,
   a patch of shadow, a fiction,
      Fortune? an illusion?
      All life is a dream
         and dreams – o'mockery –
are themselves but a dream.

from: *La Vida es Sueno*
(Life is a Dream)
Calderon

INTRODUCTION

Dreams have determined the destinies of individual lives, altered the fate of entire cultures, and been crucial to the development of Western civilization. Dreams teach, balance, inspire and heal us, and yet so many of us have forgotten the power of dreams and how they can transform our lives.

Dreams have been used throughout history as a source of creative inspiration and knowledge not normally available to the waking mind. Robert Louis Stevenson trained himself to remember his dreams, and sometimes dreamed a whole novel in one night. He wrote first for serialization in a newspaper, and took down each nightly instalment – which always came in sequence – without knowing exactly what would happen next. Even *The Strange Case of Dr Jekyll and Mr Hyde* came from Stevenson's dreams.

Charlotte Brontë used her dreams to get inside the characters she later described in her books. William Blake painted his dreams, and even learned in his dreams, through his dead brother Robert, how to engrave his designs. Poets and authors such as Wordsworth, De Quincey, Lamb, Coleridge and Edgar Allen Poe were all inspired to write by their dreams. Coleridge awoke from a dream with the complete poem of *Kubla Khan* in his head, although in the middle of writing it down he was interrupted and was never able to finish it.

Numerous dream discoveries have improved our quality of life. Otto Loewi, a Nobel Prize winner, wanted to know if nerves sent signals by transmitting electricity or by a chemical signal. He dreamed the answer, and in laboratory tests it worked. The German chemist Kekulé discovered the ring or molecular structure of benzene through his dreams, and later, while reporting his findings at a conference, said: 'Let us learn to dream, gentlemen, then we may perhaps find the truth.' The key idea for the sewing machine invented by Elias Howe came from a dream. Dreams have drastically altered the course of my own life, which would have been very different had I not followed them.

Quite recently I heard Marie Louise von Franz – both a student and a subsequent colleague of Jung's – say: 'The dream is always unique, always comes at the right moment. It is a message from the powers of the instinct, the powers of the collective unconscious, a message which comes at a specific moment, during a particular night, which is meant specifically for the dreamer.'

'The dream is always unique, always comes at the right moment.' These words are as relevant for us as they are to the great artists, writers and scientists. We, too, can learn to tap the wisdom of our dreams, which is to listen to the language of the gods. In the past, sleep was a magic state, and dreams were not only a means of curing physical and mental disorder, but also a door into the mysteries. An ancient Egyptian text says that: 'God created dreams to point out the way to the sleeper whose eyes are in darkness.' In other words, dreams can awaken us out of our unconscious sleep into a new awareness of ourselves and life.

The eminent psychologist William James said: 'I have no doubt that most people live, whether physically, intellectually or morally, in a very restricted circle of their potential being. They make use of a very small portion of their possible consciousness and of their soul's resources in general, much like a man who, out of his whole bodily organism, should get into the habit of using and moving only his little finger – we all have reservoirs of life to draw upon of which we do not dream.'

In this time of cataclysmic change, thousands of people are seeking to know more about themselves and life. Since I was a child, dreams have answered my questions, and empowered me to do many things I would not otherwise have dreamed of doing. This book is an attempt to share with you how the understanding of dreams and dream power can help everyone find meaning, purpose and fulfilment in life.

THE FIVE-POINTED STAR

The five-pointed star within a circle, also known as a pentagram, is an ancient sign symbolizing life, health and the perfected man. It is a powerful symbol of protection and, like the patterns within the Tibetan or Indian mandalas, lays a path to enlightenment. The circle represents completion, oneness with self and God, and the words inscribed around the circle are: 'In the fulfilment of the will of God lies the power of the human soul.'

To step inside the circle means that the challenges of life have pushed one to question what is life about? The pentagram mediates between inner and outer consciousness, stimulates dreams and increased awareness of ourselves and our spiritual origins.

1

DREAMS IN A TIME OF CHANGE

Economists, scientists, environmentalists, astrologers, psychics and visionaries all over the world predict that the 1990s will be the most dramatic decade in history. Warnings of ecological disaster, economic collapse, geographical upheaval, nuclear war and extraordinary genetic and technological discoveries have radically changed both life and our attitude to it. As if to confirm these predictions we have already seen changing weather patterns, earthquakes, hurricanes, holes in the ozone layer and many animal species brought to the verge of extinction, while thousands of people die daily from disease, accident and needless starvation.

Alongside such gloom and despondency, the end of the twentieth century, we are also told, heralds a new and glorious era of peace, love and understanding – a worldwide transformation of consciousness. We can see a reflection of this in the plans for a united Europe, the pulling down of the Berlin Wall, and peace negotiations between many hitherto opposed world leaders.

The world is changing so fast that many of us are finding it hard to cope. The growing dichotomy between the good and the bad is becoming more visible and confusing: a polarization of extremes is taking place both in the individual and universally. The earth is going through a huge metamorphosis, giving birth to a new age and a new form. Caught in the limbo between the death of the old and the birth of the new, we experience the pains of both. Life is not easy. This in-between state stimulates feelings of deep loneliness and pushes us to question every facet of life that we may previously have taken for granted.

The patriarchal domination of the world is coming to an end. Men and women are becoming more androgynous – a combination of male and female, neither predominant – which means that the relationship between men and women is changing. As a result the stereotyped male–female roles of the past are no longer valid. Many men today embody a stronger feminine energy and are more ready to show their feelings than in earlier generations, while many women assert and express themselves in a way previously considered to be exclusively masculine. This causes a great deal of confusion and upset, especially in matters of sexuality.·

The widespread availability of computers and advanced technology means that new generations are evolving who will never work in quite the same way as man did in the past. Ultimately this will dissolve the barrier between the left and right brain, so that we balance analytical thought with imagination and intuition, thus becoming much more creative. In the interim, however, unemployment is likely to remain a major problem. Without work, what happens to our self-worth and identity, our sense of being an integral part of society?

Taking risks

In ancient China this crucial time between the ending of one phase of civilization and the beginning of another was known as Wei Chi, which means 'moment of crisis' or 'moment of danger'. But it also means 'moment of choice' and 'opportunity for change'. Wei Chi stimulates excitement and a sense of our own power, while stirring up fear and panic – 'I can, I will, I want to' versus 'I cannot, I'll make a mistake, I'll fail'.

The choice is clearly between standing still and clinging to the apparent safety of the past, or taking the risk of leaping forward into the unknown but potentially far richer future. It is often hard to take the braver course. One of our greatest fears as human beings is that of change, of letting go, of losing hold of the familiar. Our terror of the unknown, in the form of death, may indeed prevent us from fully living and enjoying life. This fear is like that of a child who climbs so high in a tree that he is afraid to move any further, up or down. His anguished parent stands underneath with outstretched arms, crying out: 'Let go! Jump! I'll catch you!' The child knows he cannot stay where he is forever, but he clings to the security of the branch underfoot, afraid to let go in case his parent fails to catch him and he falls through the arms waiting below. Many of us are like that child. The tree is the safety and familiarity of the past. We cannot stay there, but we are afraid to jump or move on.

Encounters with danger are part of life. From them we can emerge stronger and, as from a near-death experience, with a new awareness of life. These encounters usually accompany major initiations, or shifts from one level of consciousness to another. The Wei Chi is bringing us all to the brink of an initiation so great that it is as if we were stepping from water to land for the first time. Indeed we are part of an emerging new form of life. It is imperative for the earth's future that we all jump out of our tree and participate fully in life.

The 1980s brought accelerated change, a sense of the vibratory rate of the planet speeding up. Until we adjust to it, its effects can cause chronic glandular fever-type tiredness, forgetfulness, emotional vulnerability, sleeplessness, vague cramp-like pains in the bones and joints, a sense of life getting somewhat out of control, of time shrinking, and general feelings of craziness. A reflection of this acceleration is the increasing incidence of synchronicity, the term used by the famous psychologist Carl Gustav Jung for meaningful coincidence – as when you think of a person, and they suddenly phone you.

The Influence of the Planet Pluto

The 1990s are under the influence of Pluto, a planet discovered

in 1930. Pluto rules the unconscious; it pushes forward transformation and evolution by bringing to the surface all that we
have repressed, denied or just do not want to see. Plutonian
energy stirs us to face our shadow, our ego, our past; it urges us
to live our own truth and to let go of whatever is obsolete and
outgrown. It triggers identity crises, discomfort, disruption. The
decade when Pluto was discovered ushered in an era of destruction. It was the mid-point between the two world wars; the
economy crashed; nuclear weapons were being developed; and
racism, violence and world crime increased. Pluto represents a
downward spiral of spirit into matter, into the underworld,
confrontation with fear, despair, loss and death. Pluto is the
great initiator that clears the way for new beginnings by liberat-
ing us from the past.

Instead of wringing our hands at the apparent rise of chaos
and conflict in the world, I believe that we should rejoice that all
the ills are coming to the surface so that we can see what is
confronting us. Without pain, discomfort, a lump or a rash, we
remain unaware of dis-ease. When we experience its symptoms
we do something about them.

For example, when a car engine is tuned, the rough edges are
polished so that any rusty or unfinished bits can be removed.
When we make soup stock we simmer bones in water over heat,
and gradually a froth or scum comes to the surface. Before the
heat was applied, the water looked clear. Now, when we scoop
away the surface froth, we find clear liquid underneath. In the
same way we can be brought face to face with hidden aspects of
ourselves, so that we recognize and do something about them.
Often the very fact that they are no longer hidden changes their
effect on our lives. When a pattern of behaviour is buried in our
unconscious it has power over us. When it is brought into our
consciousness we have power over it – the ability to change it.

The influence of Pluto may bring us to the dark night of the
soul which rips away the very fabric and foundation of the
persona or mask we have developed from childhood. The phrase
'dark night of the soul' comes from the writings of the sixteenth-
century Spanish mystic St John of the Cross; today it implies the
crisis when nothing that used to work for us does so any longer,

while relying solely on rational thought and external props brings us to a standstill and forces us either to scream for help to something beyond ourselves, or to look within and delve deeply into our unconscious. This crisis assists evolution by stimulating a re-evaluation of past, present and future, of our relationship to everyone and everything around us. A near-death experience does exactly the same thing. For many people it provides the opportunity to change their entire attitude to life.

The Fisher King Legend

We are all suffering – the literal meaning of the word is to 'undergo' – an identity crisis, a planetary near-death experience, stimulated by the earth herself. By manifesting symptoms of disease, she forces us to look at our relationship with all of life. Rather like children of school age, who are characteristically selfish and self-conscious, we are now moving on to university to graduate and develop cosmic consciousness. In the process we must heal what is called the Fisher King wound, which continues to plague many people all over the world.

This concept comes from the centuries-old story of Parsifal and the quest for the Holy Grail. Today it symbolizes the state of being in which we have access to virtually all the world's riches and knowledge of which we can conceive – including a technology that can send men to the moon and the bottom of the ocean, can transplant organs and prolong life after brain death, and can show us what is happening in every corner of the globe merely by the flick of a switch on a television set – yet in which our life simply does not work. We are dysfunctional, unhappy and unfulfilled. We are unable to express our creativity, joy or spontaneity. We do not enjoy or celebrate life.

The tale starts with the arrival in a wood of the Fisher King, then a boy about twelve years old. He finds the embers of a fire, still glowing hot, and the remains of a fish on a spit above it. He picks up the spit, which is so hot that he drops it. It pierces his thigh and wounds him, and from that moment he is unable to walk. The story says that he can only be healed by a naïve and innocent fool. Meanwhile the land he rules is also afflicted – the crops will not grow and the sun does not shine.

The story is relevant for anyone who during childhood, especially at pre-teen age, experienced something so traumatic that on some level they switched off. Part of my own Fisher King wound was caused by the nuns at my convent school forcing me to stand in front of five hundred girls at morning prayers while they declared: 'Your mother is a sinner because she is divorced, which makes you a sinner too. Now, girls, this is what a sinner looks like.' I did not even know what a sinner was. I only knew I was one, so I played the fool and pretended that I didn't care, and so became virtually unteachable. I imagine that as a young schoolboy Jung received a Fisher King wound when he wrote such a brilliant essay that the teacher assumed he must have copied it. Instead of discussing it with Jung, the teacher read aloud to the entire school what every other boy had written. Finally he said of Jung's work: 'This is so outstanding that it must have been copied. Because I don't know the source of his information all I can do is to leave it unread.' Jung was devastated, never forgave his teacher and 'switched off' to normal education.

The Fisher King wound can be the result of rape, incest, death, loss, a sudden change in environment, even from falling in love (especially when mocked by the family) with the girl next door. In fact it can come from anything that forces us to 'close off' emotionally.

Many of us also have a father/mother wound that triggers a lack of trust in our own male/female energy. The male drive is what we use to express ourselves in life. It is outgoing, active and creative. We use its power to run, walk, talk, scrub a floor, make love, paint a picture or write a book. Female energy is ingoing, receptive. We use it to listen, think, imagine, feel, intuit. Our relationship with our inner man and woman is modelled on the attitude of our father and mother to each other, as well as to us, during childhood. If on some level our mother is 'not there' for us, we will not trust our feelings, imagination or intuition.

We will hold back from 'heartfully' relating to others and there-fore to life itself. If the father was 'not there', the energy of the inner man will not be there either. To compensate, we will then become either extremely hard-working, competitive, conscien-tious perfectionists, or procrastinators and start-stoppers who can never get anything done. Because I neither saw nor had any kind of contact with my father from the age of six, and had a somewhat absent relationship with my mother, I am all too familiar with these inhibiting patterns of behaviour.

When the Parsifal legend says that the Fisher King can be healed by a naïve and innocent fool, it means that, no matter how frozen and wounded we are, we can still heal and free ourselves. To do so we have to listen to the child within, heal that child and let the joyous, spontaneous part of us speak out. The story also stresses that the only relief the Fisher King can get from his pain and paralysis comes from fishing alone in a boat. In other words, in spite of his inability to walk or to express himself as a man (the wound was in his groin) he can still fish freely and productively through the waters of the emotions and the subconscious, and delve even more deeply into the unconscious.

Parsifal, the naive and innocent child of the story, seeks the Grail – his soul – and, to save the Fisher King, must ask the question, 'Whom does the Grail serve?' The answer is that it serves the Grail King or God. Similarly, as soon as we pose the question, 'What is life about?' – meaning that there must be a purpose beyond earning a living, having a house and a car, and educating one's children – life changes, and we begin to connect to both life purpose and soul purpose. (Soul purpose is reunion with God, and life purpose what we do to achieve it.)

If we do not ask this question, for fear of the demands which the answer may make on us, we stay locked in a useless and frustrating immobility. It is no good lamenting, 'If only I knew what to do, I would do it.' We have within us everything we need to fulfil our destinies. We must remember that, no matter how difficult life may appear, we can, and indeed must, delve like the Fisher King deeply into our unconscious, where we may well find all the answers we require. In *Modern Man in Search of a Soul* Jung wrote: 'If it were possible to personify the unconscious we might call it a collective human being combining the characteristics of both sexes, transcending youth and age, birth and death, and from having at his command a human experience of one or two million years – almost immortal.'

With such a source of wisdom, inspiration, healing and balance within us, how sad it is that most of us struggle blindly through life without making any attempt to get in touch with it, especially as it is made available to us every night when we sleep, through our dreams.

As adults, most of us exist cut off from the unconscious, which contains a cast of characters symbolizing myriad hidden aspects of ourselves, and which presents information to us in a rich, colourful language of image and symbol. If we learn to communicate with these images and understand their meaning, we can assimilate into our waking lives the energies they represent and become more wise and whole, in the sense of being united with all our parts. This enables us to enjoy much freer and happier lives. As an example, people who dream and imagine a wide variety of sexual relationships without guilt or censorship tend to be more creative in every area of waking life, and not just on a sexual level.

The Value of the Imagination

Imagination comes from the Latin word *imago*, which means image. Imagination is the channel between conscious and unconscious; it converts what is invisible information into images so we can see and learn to understand. During the day, the unconscious makes its presence felt in the form of moods, feelings, flashes of intuition, daydreams and fantasies. At night the unconscious uses the imagination to create the pictures which form our dreams.

Imagination, therefore, is the way to the unconscious, and dreams are the most perfect means of learning its language.

Unfortunately, during childhood most of us are taught to deny the value of our imagination. We are frequently told: 'It's only your imagination', as if this were something to be ashamed of.

When I was a child I saw the life force and inner essence of everything around me. Flowers, trees, plants, rocks and stones spoke to me. I saw thoughts, words and feelings flying around as streams of colours and energy. Faces, figures and shapes appeared and disappeared. I saw past, present and future happening simultaneously and apparently solid matter such as houses, tables and chairs suddenly dissolve into vibrating atoms in front of me. I felt as if everything was in constant, flowing movement, and that I was part of a vast cosmic dance whose story I must tell.

I began to write stories about what I saw, and to talk to imaginary friends who were much more companionable than my brother, who bit me and stole my toys. As a result I was told, 'You're making this up!' or 'You're far too imaginative!', while other people were told: 'Don't take her seriously – she imagines things', as if I were retarded. I was punished not physically, but by disapproval. Without knowing exactly what I had done I felt guilty, ashamed, afraid of myself and very secretive about my perceptions, which I tried to stifle (with disastrous results later in my life). Children must be encouraged to use their imagination and taught to develop it as a wonderful key that facilitates the exploration of our inner space.

Some years ago I was working in America with Paul Solomon, the American healer, teacher and mystic. We told a group of brain-damaged eight-year-olds: 'There's nothing wrong with you, but you've got cobwebs in your brains. We're going to show you how to scrub your brains with soap and water and wash the cobwebs away.' Three times a day for seven days these children sat with their eyes tightly closed, and imagined that they were pouring buckets of water over their heads and scrubbing their brains with a brush. They loved it: we treated it as a game and there was much laughter. After seven days the brain damage had not changed, but the children's attitude had. Instead of 'I can't' they now said 'I can', and began to learn new skills. We even taught footballers in Virginia to rehearse each game in their imaginations before they played against other teams who were trained normally – simply on a football field. In each match the team which had been 'training in their heads' won.

But since the time of the Greek philosopher Aristotle, who believed that everything we do, think and feel should be under rational control, and that logic should be used to direct and guide man's natural instincts, the Western world has virtually ignored the power of the right brain and depended exclusively on the logical thinking of the left brain. Many of us have in this way become half-wits. Because computers and high technology are taking over much of what man formerly did with his left brain, he now has at his disposal infinitely more mental energy to devote to developing his right. It is through the right brain that we can create links between different levels of consciousness. We can now, like the Fisher King in the Parsifal legend, go fishing, or, even better, launch ourselves like Columbus into a magnificent voyage of discovery. Dreams and the imagination are the means by which the invisible becomes visible. By paying attention to our dreams, by listening to our dreams, we can safely chart the unknown seas of our inner selves.

The Great Dream Interpreters

Some of the greatest and most original minds in human history, including Freud, Jung and Edgar Cayce, have been fascinated by dreams. Dreams were described by Sigmund Freud as 'the royal road to the unconscious'. In 1900, after years of studying his own and many other people's dreams, he published his book *The Interpretation of Dreams*. He shocked Europe by suggesting that the unconscious was a cesspool of many things we do not admit into our waking minds. He believed that buried impulses, such as repressed memories, censored – and probably incestuous – desires, primitive impulses and thoughts that we might judge shameful when awake, resulted in dreams that attempted to resolve these issues. Freud was medically and scientifically trained. He believed that you could not separate the dream from the dreamer, nor the mind of the dreamer from his dream; the two must always be seen in relationship to each other. Probably his most important contribution to the understanding of dreams was his exposition of the dream as a source of research.

Carl Jung, who was once a student of Freud's, believed that all his own work and creativity, everything that he accomplished over the next fifty years, came from his dreams and fantasies which began in 1912. Even before he met Freud, Jung regarded dreams as an important element in the balance of the human psyche. He believed that dreaming was as important to the wellbeing of 'normal people' as it was to the mentally disturbed. Thus a dream was not merely a symptom of neurosis as it was for Freud.

The ideas of both Freud and Jung have had a profound effect on our attitude to dreams today, which I shall discuss further in Chapter 6. Meanwhile I believe that the basic difference in their work is that Freud looked at what the dream might conceal, while Jung looked at what it might reveal.

On the other side of the globe, at about the same time that Jung was making his discoveries in the early part of the century, another man from a much simpler educational background and a totally different standpoint was reaching similar conclusions about the nature of dreams and the unconscious. Even today, long after his death, Edgar Cayce is probably still researched and written about more than any other psychic/trance medium who has ever lived. While in a sleep or trance state he could see into the past and the future; he accurately diagnosed illness and the necessary treatment for thousands of people. His readings – words spoken while he was in this trance state – were transcribed and carefully documented. The ARE (Association of Research and Enlightenment) was founded in Virginia Beach, Virginia in 1931 to study and disseminate the information that Edgar Cayce gave.

Instead of Jung's collective unconscious Cayce referred to the collective or universal subconscious, which he saw 'as a river of thought fed by the sum total of man's mental activity since his beginning'. He maintained that this river is accessible to anyone who is prepared, patiently and systematically, to develop his psychic or spiritual faculties. In one reading Cayce said: 'Dreams are a manifestation of the subconscious. Any condition before becoming a reality is first dreamed.'

Since I was a child dreams have played a vital role in my life, and therefore, during my first visit to work with Paul Solomon in America, I went as soon as I could to the ARE to explore some of Edgar Cayce's work. Solomon has been compared to Cayce because their 'breakthrough' into altered states of consciousness came about in a similar manner. Both were at a standstill in their lives, both were hypnotized, and in each case a 'voice spoke through' them during their first hypnotic sessions, giving specific instructions as to what must be done to effect a cure. When Solomon developed his psychic ability he had never heard of Edgar Cayce, although by the time I went to America he was living in Virginia Beach too. I found the parallels between the two men extraordinary, and consider myself lucky to have had access to the wisdom of both.

In a reading given by Solomon on the subject of dreams he said: 'Dreams are acts of the soul assessing how we handle the lessons of the day, recording these assessments on the Akashic record' (the record of everything since the beginning of time – similar to Jung's collective unconscious and Cayce's 'river of thought'), 'and then reflecting them back to the conscious mind.' In other words, according to Solomon, dreams are like a mirror and show us how we are proceeding through life, where we are doing well, where we are falling down and how we could do better.

What Dreams Reveal

Of course dreams are all of this and very much more. Dreams can heal, teach, warn, guide, prophesy, answer questions, connect us to past, present and future, provide us with amusement and pleasure, bring emotional balance, stimulate creativity and sexuality, solve problems, prepare us for the unknown and enable us to live out unlived parts of ourselves. Through dreams we are shown that, as Shakespeare said, 'All the world's a stage, and all the men and women on it merely players....' Day and night we play a multitude of parts – observers one minute, participants the next. In the process we are reminded that each individual life is our own movie, the result of our own creativity. We write our own dramas, we produce, direct and act in them, and we have the power to improve the script if it is not a box-office success.

Because of a dream, while driving a car at 90 mph down a major highway in the Australian outback, with my child, parrot and basset hound in the back, I suddenly remembered to slow down. Seconds later the tyre burst and we zigzagged all over the road: at 90 mph we would all have been killed.

Another dream showed me driving over a bridge which collapsed as I was halfway across it. The sensation of the road giving way under the car, and of falling into the water below amidst tons of crashing masonry, was so strong that the following day when I found myself driving towards a bridge over water I turned away and took another route. The next day there were headlines in the paper: 'Bridge collapses. Many dead.'

A dream stopped a friend of mine from getting on a South African Airways plane that crashed in Mauritius with no survivors. The night before the major fire at London's King's Cross Underground Station another friend dreamed that the taxi she had taken to the station refused to stop and drove straight past. The following evening, instead of coming home via King's Cross she took a taxi all the way and avoided what she later learned was a disaster.

Maggie dreamed that her eleven-year-old son Nick, who was at boarding school, had run away and was wandering around wretched and desperate in an area of wild country not far from home. Because she was already uneasy as to whether boarding school was the best place for him, she lay awake thinking that the dream had come out of her own anxiety. Of course it had –

but there was more to it than that. At 9 a.m. the school telephoned to say that Nick had run away. She got in her car, drove to the area where she had seen her son in her dream, and found him.

These were all precognitive dreams, but not all dreams are like that. Some give us a nudge to change direction, such as those experienced by St Francis of Assisi, who set off to fight in the wars but had dreams which turned him back. Tom saw himself climbing a mountain from which he fell when he reached the top. It put him in touch with his driving ambition, which was literally leading him to a dead end.

Other dreams prepare us for death, loss and change. Before his assassination Abraham Lincoln saw a coffin guarded by soldiers and surrounded by weeping people.

'Who is dead?' he asked.

'The President, killed by an assassin,' was the reply.

Many people predicted President Kennedy's death. They included one woman who telephoned the White House the previous day to say that she had dreamt that Kennedy would be killed in Dallas.

Although I barely knew my father, three days before his death I dreamed that I saw him laid out in white naval uniform (he had in fact been an officer in the Royal Navy in World War II) on a barge, which stopped alongside the river bank on which I stood. I looked at him for what seemed a long time, and felt such a sense of peace that it made the past irrelevant. I was not surprised when the news of his death came.

Susan, dying of cancer and fearing the moment of death, dreamed she saw the flickering flame of a candle gradually being extinguished. Believing that this symbolized her own life drawing to a close she awoke, feeling a deep sadness. After some time she drifted back to sleep and saw the flame reignite outside the window, this time burning with far more radiance than before. She felt she had been shown a continuity of existence on the 'other side' which alleviated her fear. Within twenty-four hours of her dream she died peacefully.

My own dreams have helped me to change jobs and to stop eating certain foods that it later turned out I was allergic to.

They have also shown me what to do to help a friend whose son had been murdered, and another who was dying of cancer.

To listen and pay attention to dreams, and above all to take appropriate action afterwards, connects us to a wiser, more intelligent self than the one we usually know and use, and to an energy that empowers us to behave differently. For example, during a workshop I held in South Africa a woman asked me what she could do to help her eight-year-old son who suffered from recurring nightmares. These were traumatic not only for the boy but also for the entire family, who were woken by his screams. I suggested that the next time he had the nightmare she should encourage him to face the monster, point his finger or a crystal at it, and, while imagining light or colour directed at it, shrink it until it was small enough to pick up. He could then ask the monster its name and make friends with it. To the family's amazement, the child remembered to do this and ran into breakfast talking excitedly about his new friend and what they were planning to do together that night. He never had the nightmare again.

Two days later his mother had a nightmare in which an enormous figure in scuba-diving equipment climbed through her bedroom window. Waking in panic, her heart thumping, she remembered her son's nightmare and what he had done to clear it. She closed her eyes, imagined pointing a finger at her own monster, and was astonished when it shrank into a knee-high dwarf wearing a red woolly hat and boots, who then scurried out of the room. She told me later: 'I was *not* asleep when I pointed my finger – I simply imagined doing it. How can something change like that when I don't really believe it will work?'

The family lived on a farm in an isolated area about a hundred miles from Johannesburg, and the following week her husband was away on business. In the middle of the night a sudden noise at her bedroom window woke her up. She opened her eyes to find a large man climbing in. Before she could scream, run or even move in the bed, he was beside her with a knife at her throat. She shrank down in the bed, shivering with fright, convinced that she was about to die.

Unexpectedly, the memory of her dream returned. In spite of

her fear, it gave her the courage to sit up, point her finger at the man and say: 'How *dare* you speak to me like this? Drop that knife at once and leave my house immediately!' The man was so shocked by the sudden change in her that he drew back, dropped the knife and ran from the room.

Her nightmare was a precognitive warning dream. It enabled her to have a dress rehearsal for the real event and connected her to a part of herself that knew what to do. Because she faced the threat and did something about it in the dream, she was empowered to move from reaction to action in 'real' life.

The Power to Change Lives

When we work with dreams we draw their energy into our lives and become infinitely more effective people. Life changes dramatically. Children who learn to shrink monsters to a huggable size in their dreams and imagination grow into adults who shrink life's problems to a manageable size by fearlessly facing them.

The power of the unconscious to transform our lives is truly incredible. When Paul Solomon had his second mystic experience he was surrounded by a small group of very curious people. They had been told of the voice that spoke through him when he was in a sleep or trance, and which gave highly specific instructions on how to improve the quality of his life. They wanted to know who or what this voice was. As soon as Paul lay down and closed his eyes the voice spoke again and, when asked 'Who are you?' said, 'I am the source of Paul's intelligence, a part of Paul's consciousness that knows everything from the beginning of time.' They then asked if this intelligence was unique to Paul because he was a genius, and were told very firmly, 'No. This intelligence is available to every single human being, but most are either unaware of it or unable to contact it.' Later this voice became known as 'the source', and it is what Paul links into every time he does a reading.

This intelligent soul or source part of our minds is like a teacher or an older brother or sister who knows more than we do. It is similar to Jung's 'collective human being', androgynous, with millions of years of human experience. If, as I and many others believe, life is a school and we are the students, does it not make sense to get in touch with the teacher, who no doubt sets the lessons, knows the answers and has already been trying to communicate with us through dreams since we were born? Instead of wringing our hands and crying, 'Woe is me! Why do all these things keep happening to me? What have I done to deserve this?' we can find out. We can ask the teacher. Imagination, visualization and especially meditation are ways of picking up the telephone to dial the teacher's number. However, many of us have forgotten the exact number to dial. Dreams are the telephone call from the teacher to us, which most of us never hear. To watch and listen to our dreams is a simple, safe and powerful way of picking up the telephone and answering the call.

The Route to Inner Wisdom

This time of crisis, of Wei Chi, the energies of the final decade of this century, are pushing us to stop looking outside for the answers and to dive into inner space where the answers are waiting to be found. Dreams are the magic route to this inner wisdom. An old legend says that when the gods created the human race they argued about where to put the secrets of life so that they would not be found too easily. One god wanted to put them on the top of a mountain, another in the centre of the earth, while yet another said: 'Put them at the bottom of the sea. They'll never find them there.' No matter what was suggested, they could not agree. At last one of the gods said: 'Let's put this knowledge *inside* them. They'll never look there!' It's time we proved them wrong.

2

HOW DREAMS
HELP US

The Power of Dreams in My Life

All my life I have dreamt and remembered my dreams. When I
was a little girl in Sri Lanka, my nights were peopled with faces,
figures and outstretched arms waiting to grab me when I fell out
of bed. The recurring nightmares in which I lay on fat pink
writhing snakes caused me to toss and turn in terror. I fell out of
bed almost every night, but before I hit the floor I was caught by
the mosquito netting protecting me. I hung passively for what
seemed an eternity, afraid to call out because this would bring
my ayah – my nurse – who would beat me for waking her.

My subsequent life and work would have been very different
without what I consider to be an indestructible link between my
inner and outer worlds. Both meditation and dreams have been
the way in to a part of myself that has access to a far greater
wisdom than that of my everyday, waking self. Dreams,
however, were important to me long before I heard of meditation, let alone began to practise it. Dreams allowed me to see
my own myths and helped me find my place in the world.
Dreams encouraged me to move out of being an accident-prone,
self-pitying victim and say: 'I will participate in the game of life
even if it hurts.'

And dreams can do this for everyone. Dreams are a bridge, a communication, a letter from the soul; they are a source of power, knowledge, creativity and health. If we ignore dreams we deprive ourselves of the intelligence that, as the Paul Solomon source said, 'is available to every single human being, but most are either unaware of it or unable to contact it'.

We do not have to be psychic, clairvoyant or telepathic to be in touch with this intelligence. All we have to do is listen – to our intuition, our imagination, and especially to our dreams. Dreams are the language of the gods – a language rich in meaning and metaphor, individually tailored to wake us from sleep into life. Like any language, the more we immerse ourselves in it the more understandable it becomes, and suddenly our lives begin to change. We stop behaving like sleep-walkers, people who live on 'automatic pilot', without thought or reflection, and wake up. We become conscious and aware. As we live that awareness, we cease to be helpless victims of a capricious fate, and move into mastery of life.

A lifetime's dreaming

The dreams of my early childhood continued. But in spite of the traumas I loved going to bed because of the adventures I had. As my eyes closed, bare-breasted women draped in intricate bead-work, with naked black babies strapped to their backs, rose up against a landscape of African huts. Egyptian princesses, finely boned and wearing exotic head-dresses, with tall, dark Pharoahs beside them, floated past sand-strewn pyramids. Unicorns cavorted and gambolled through brilliant green meadows before lifting into the sky to swing through the clouds, sometimes taking me with them.

All these scenes were hypnagogic images – the pictures and faces which frequently appear in our mind's eye, sometimes as clearly as if projected on to a screen in front of us, as we relax into sleep or begin to wake up. I enjoyed them, and still do, just as I enjoy going to the movies. However, what I really looked forward to all day, what was my comfort in an insecure child-hood, was that night after night I flew with a star-spangled fairy who, with a wave of her wand, lifted me over the house, the palm trees and rice paddies, up and up into the sky where the shadowy shapes of the dark could never reach me. We soared through the air, drifted and glided, dancing through the night so safe and free that I thought I would never feel afraid or lonely again. We played with rainbows and sang to the sun; we dangled from clouds and rode unicorns bareback. I often 'became' the unicorn, and felt the physical sensation of having hooved feet and a horn protruding from my head. As we lifted into the air or galloped up mountains, the horn dissolved into a ring of jewels in the centre of my forehead. Colours and flowers cascaded around us. We flew with flamingoes, went fishing with pelicans, swam with huge turtles and chatted with parrots.

These dreams were so vivid and full of excitement and joy that even today they stay in my memory as if they were real events. Such magical flights richly made up for my everyday fears. As a result, I learned from a very early age to value my dreams and their power to affect my life. When I was about six I began to write some of them down as if they were stories. I still do so today. I discovered that if I had questions about almost any aspect of life a dream would give me the answer, and much of what I have learnt has come through dreams.

The Power of the Sun

Apart from my flying fairy friend, who as I grew up turned into a winged guardian angel, the sun too featured prominently in my childhood dreams. I saw it as a great glowing orb, in the centre of which was a triangle containing an eye that 'saw everything'. Sometimes the triangle became a huge radiant figure from which streams of light flowed, bringing life in the form of rocks, trees, plants, flowers and water to the earth wherever they touched it. At other times I found myself looking *into* the eye, which then became a door leading into another sun, and then another and another. To walk into the innermost heart of the sun was like merging with the red heat of a fiery furnace, yet without being burnt.

Not only was I shown the sun as a manifestation of the light of God, and taught to honour and revere it, but I also seemed to experience its rhythms of expansion and contraction, sunrise and sunset. It was almost as if the sun had swallowed me, and I had swallowed the sun. I was born on Sunday at sunrise, and have often dreamt of being carried into life on the crest of the sun's rays. Dreams in which the sun appears are always highly significant for me.

For example, when I was writing my first book, *The Power of Gems and Crystals*, I looked forward to finishing it and expected to feel a sense of relief and exhilaration when I did. Instead I was surprised to find myself depressed and uneasy, a little like a woman who has given birth to a baby, and, after months of anticipation, suddenly wonders what all the fuss was about. That same night, I dreamed that the sun came into my room through the ceiling, a glowing sphere of fire. Rays of golden orange poured into me; every cell in my body came alive. I stood with my arms outstretched, and suddenly from the centre of the sun a great ball of light came into my hands. As I held it a voice said: 'This is all you need – the language of light. You need no other. You must take this light and shine it wherever you go. Use it in all that you do.' The effect was so electrifying that it woke me up. It was 3 a.m. but I leaped out of bed bursting with energy and eager to get on with my life.

A few hours later there was a knock on the door. I opened it and saw my friend Val standing there; she pushed a huge crystal ball into my hands. It gleamed and shone as if lit up from within, and it had the same effect on my body as the ball of sunlight had had in the dream: I thought I would burst out of my skin. I felt intoxicated, not merely from the power pulsing through the crystal, but also because this was outer confirmation of the inner message in the dream: a meaningful coincidence that Jung would have called synchronicity.

A *source of energy and intelligence*

The sun has been more than just a powerful force in my dreams. I grew up with the ability to 'see' – to shift focus into other realities or to 'tune in' to different vibratory fields of existence, as if I were tuning in to different channels on the radio or TV. I had no control over this; it was as if a switch went on or off in my brain. I learned that it was something to keep very quiet about, and I became both confused and a little afraid of myself. Because I saw the sun as a living force of energy and intelligence, I often spoke to it; and I felt that it sometimes 'lit up' in reply and winked at me. At these times even my 'drifting into sleep' hypnagogic images became little round golden yellow smiling sun-like faces. As a result, later on in my life I often asked the sun for a sign or proof that my perceptions were valid, and that they were not coming out of an unlived fragment of my own subconscious – an unexpressed part of myself.

On one occasion, while climbing Mount Shasta in California with a mediumistic friend who began to channel information which made me feel uncomfortable, I looked to the sun to confirm or negate my own thoughts. We were on a broad ledge which had an uncanny atmosphere of other-worldly peace. A sixty-foot tree had split in half and fallen to lie like an altar to Pan. Moss-green grass grew underfoot, and a deer stood quivering in the shadows beyond the fallen tree. While my friend slept, I said to the sun: 'Show me the truth.' Words exploded in my head, denying what my friend had said. I then asked the sun: 'If this is of truth, of God, not of my personality, let the sun move!'

To my everlasting amazement, the sun moved quite decisively across the sky. Stunned, I decided that the blur of sunlight in my eyes had affected my vision. I stared at the shadows on the ground. If the sun really moved, the shadows would move too. As long as I looked at the ground my eyes could not be dazzled again. I placed a handkerchief, a comb, a coin, twigs and grass to mark the shadows' lines on the ground, and asked the sun to move again. I watched the ground. The shadows leaped about six feet to the left. Shocked, in that instant I made decisions which profoundly affected my life.

A week later, on my way back to England, I decided to visit the Meditation Room of the United Nations Building in New York. This is a small, enclosed room without windows, pervaded with an atmosphere of peace which is a delightful contrast to the hustle and bustle of city life going on outside. Arriving early, I waited on the ground floor for the Meditation Room to be opened. I was standing next to a window that faced on to a vast expanse of brick wall. Suddenly the sun flooded the room, almost blinding me, pinning me to the spot until the guard arrived to take me into the room. There was no way in which the sun could have shone through the window in that manner.

The sun has long been revered as a source of divine revelation and spiritual experience. Primitive rock engravings show circles and wheels long before the wheel was invented. Some of these engravings depict circles, each of which has a dot in the centre. In my mandala work today, which involves interpreting what people draw inside a circle, I would interpret this configuration as a symbol of the whole and centred self.

Many ancient cults and religions believed that the sun was the creative masculine principle of God, while the moon represented the feminine equivalent. Sun worship was a means of discovering the source of life and light, and could lead to enlightenment. Ceremonies dedicated to the sun and celebrating its life-giving power, such as the American Indian sun-dance, are still performed today. Great civilizations such as those of the Babylonians, Aztecs, Mayas, Egyptians and Greeks worshipped the sun, and so did primitive indigenous peoples. The Greeks worshipped Apollo as their sun god, while in Egypt he was called Ra and one of the sun symbols was the golden scarab. The pyramids supposedly reflect the sun's rays expanding out from the high heavens to the earth, and drawings in ancient Egyptian papyruses illustrate worship of the Sun Tree from the legend of Hathor, who gave birth to the sun. The boy king Tutankhamun is often pictured enthroned against the background of a golden sun disc, whose beams stream down ending in open hands symbolizing the sun's life-giving force. Some indigenous tribes believe that to dream of the sun means that the dreamer has predominantly masculine qualities, while to dream of the moon means the reverse. In Joan Halifax's book *Shamanic Voices* she writes of a shaman – a medicine man – in the Mexican Sierras who says: 'You must listen to the fire, for the fire speaks and the fire teaches, and during the day you learn from the sun. The sun will teach you.' The sun has taught me a great deal. I believe that it speaks and will speak to you if you are willing to listen.

Sun worship

In *Woman's Mysteries*, Esther Harding writes that moon worship was superseded by sun worship at the same time that male power and the patriarchal system began to rise. Moon worship was concerned with the unseen powers of the spirit, while worship of the sun was the worship of the capacity to achieve, conquer and bring order out of chaos. The moon is the ruler of the night, of the unconscious. She is what the Chinese call the Yin or receptive principle; the sun is Yang, the outgoing or active principle, who rules the day, work and consciousness.

Apart from my own sun dreams and experiences, I have also practised sun worship as taught by the Bulgarian teacher Peter Deunov, or Beinsa Douna as he is usually known. Although he died in 1944 and therefore I have not met him in a physical sense, he has profoundly influenced my life. Visions and dreams in which he appeared aroused in me the desire to visit Bulgaria and make contact with those who were left from the esoteric school that he founded at the turn of the century. These dreams and visions have continued to pull me to the Bulgarian mountains every summer, where the daily discipline is to rise between 3.30 and 4 a.m. and climb to a peak known as the Sphinx to greet the sun.

Beinsa Douna taught that the sun was a manifestation of God, and that in order to feel physically, mentally and spiritually healthy one should align with the rhythm of sunrise and sunset.

The Power of the Moon

Although for me the sun is more significant than the moon, I have always experienced strong emotions and strange dreams when the moon is full. In one such dream I felt myself soaring from the sky and hanging from the moon while the earth lay far below. A strong male voice said: 'This is to remind you of the quantum leap in consciousness you must make in order to take your next step in life – you think you've made one before, but nothing like the quantum leap you must make now.' My moon dreams have certainly affected me and I have felt empowered by them, but they do not awaken me with the same jolt as when I dream of the sun.

The moon rules the night and the unconscious; its power as a source of inspiration, fantasy, intuition and dreams has long been known and worshipped. Because the moon reflects the hidden light of the sun, it seems to draw the hidden, instinctual aspects of ourselves to the surface, causing emotional upheaval and confusion, uncontrollable outbursts, or withdrawal and introspection. Nightmares and suicides are more common during the phase of the full moon, while animals are often restless by its light. The power of the moon liberates us from the construction of the mind, stirs up the unconscious and so stimulates 'lunatic' behaviour – lunacy aptly describes emotions out of control and comes from the Latin word 'luna'.

According to Plutarch, Egyptian priests styled the moon '"The Mother of the Universe" because the moon having the light which makes moist and pregnant is promotive of the generation of living beings and the fructification of plants'. They were right. Think of the early morning dew refreshing, nurturing and nourishing plants. 'Moist and pregnant' is what the earth becomes under the influence of the moon.

Many ancient religions believed that the moon represented the feminine principle of God. They often defined the moon as a trinity of Moon Maiden, Mother/Queen and old crone, each reflecting a different phase of waxing and waning. Dreams, too, respond to the phases of the moon.

Astarte, the Greek equivalent of Isis, was believed to hold the power of life, death and health for men and gods. Although she was known as the Moon Goddess, festivals celebrating the different phases were dedicated to Selene (full moon), Aphrodite (bright moon), Hecate (dark or waning moon), Artemis (crescent moon) and Cybele (Hecate's successor), as well as to Astarte herself. The bright moon was 'good and kind', gave inspiration, understanding, dreams and visions, while her dark side created havoc, such as storms, crisis and emotional upset – think about lunatics and lunacy.

Priestesses dedicated to the moon's service performed rites to ensure the earth's fertility, and kept alight a sacred flame symbolizing the moon's rays. Men who wanted to partake of the nature of the Moon Goddess would come to the temple and sexually unite with the priestess who was in that moment her representative. For men outside the temple, this initiation was usually done only once in a lifetime, in an act of surrender to the goddess and all she symbolized.

The Babylonians were also moon worshippers. They worshipped the moon more than the sun, and believers in prophetic dreams said that if a man dreamed of his own image in the moon he would become father of a son. Conversely a woman dreaming of her image in the moon would give birth to a daughter.

In the past, many people believed that a baby could only be born on an incoming tide and a person reaching the end of life could only die when the tide went out. As the moon governs the ocean's tides, so she was supposed to govern the ebb and flow of life and death.

Dreams with a Message

Dreams can still have a dramatic impact even if they do not feature the sun or moon. During a particularly traumatic phase of my life, when day after day I felt as if I were suffocating in thick, black fog, I dreamed I was dragging my body inch by inch up a mountain made of huge, rough steps. Each step was as tall as my body: I could reach the next one only by standing on tiptoe and straining to get my fingertips over the edge. By the time I reached the top my body was raw and bleeding. Confronting me was a thick, shapeless mass of black, evil-looking slime. I knew it was the sum total of all that had happened and all my fears of what might happen.

Revolted, I turned to go back down the mountain but was too afraid of the height. Transfixed with fear I turned to face the blackness, and almost involuntarily my fist smashed into it. What had been thick, dark slime exploded into thousands of glittering crystal rainbows that arced through the air, scattering light and colour all around me.

The effect of the dream was like receiving an electric shock or jump-starting a car with a flat battery. It forced me to face my fears and my life. After months of retreat I got out of bed and filled the house with flowers. I recognized that, as long as I turned my back on the dark, it grew. When I confronted it, I mastered it.

Another dynamic dream came for a very different reason. I was at the time totally immersed in spiritual work, giving classes on meditation, dreams, stress release, relationships, journal writing, healing, the use of crystals, colour and sound. Much of this took place during residential workshops and seminars. It involved getting up at dawn to share breathing and relaxation exercises before pre-breakfast meditation; then there were day and evening classes. After the evening class question time would often continue until the early hours of the morning, and I began to feel like a twenty-four-hour-a-day nun without benefit of a cell into which to retreat. I was never alone; even my room was shared with others.

One day, after travelling around the world in this way, a part of me rebelled. At 2 a.m. I went outside and shouted to the heavens: 'I've got nothing left, do you hear? Everyone and everything I valued in my life has gone. Even my clothes are second-hand – do you want these too?' I tore off my dress and flung it to the ground. Then I paced up and down, shaking my fist at the sky, seething with rebellion and fury.

Expecting the skies to fall in, I picked up my dress and went to bed, where I dreamed I was lifted to a very high place. The air was uncannily pure and light. I sensed an invisible figure beside me. Far below, amongst rocks and boulders, I saw a dark pit in which creatures, half human, half feathered and furred, were tearing lumps out of one another. I felt a pain so great I thought my heart would burst open, and recognized that the scene symbolized what human beings do to one another. I floated down into the pit, smelling blood, hearing cries and screams, and saw feathers, flesh and fur ripped off in chunks. A voice said: 'Well. . . .'

Suddenly the scene changed. I was now standing on emerald green grass, looking at a huge wooden wheel, its rim balanced in the earth. People were tied to the spokes like little rag dolls. As the wheel turned, dragging them into the earth, their arms and legs flailed wildly about. Again I felt a piercing pain in my heart. I saw the words 'wheel of karma' and knew that I must help these people face and understand the laws of karma – laws of cause and effect – and so get off the wheel. My pain changed to intense love and compassion, while my mind became clinically detached.

I was then taken through what seemed to be every inch of my life. One experience after another – bad, sad, tragic or funny – rose in front of my eyes with a complete understanding of why it had had to be like that. I saw myself like a spoilt child, stamping my foot and yelling: 'I'm not going to do this any more!' Then a giant hand picked me up by the scruff of my neck and its owner said: 'Look at this – and this – and this. What do you think you've been trained for? Whom does your life serve?' I woke up with every cell in my body buzzing. I had total clarity about why my life had been as it had. I felt completely revitalized in my sense of mission, and from that time on I have never again turned away from my work.

For me the guarantee of a dream's importance is both the emotional impact within the dream and the electrifying burst of energy with which I wake up to implement the dream's message. Even without specific interpretation, I believe a dream has been truly understood and integrated when one's life changes as a result.

3

THE LOST CHILD

The exotic flights of fantasy that coloured my childhood dreams were, as I said in Chapter 2, a form of escape from a not very happy childhood. Many of us either had unhappy times in our childhoods or suffered a Fisher King wound of the kind I talked about earlier. Later in life, we can use dreams to help us confront and handle these situations in retrospect. They can help us change our lives.

All my work, whether it's using dreams, hands, crystals, visualizations or deep relaxation techniques, is about helping people to find the *cause* of a problem, illness or dis-ease, and treating *it* rather than treating the symptom. If you can treat the cause, the symptom tends to go away. I help people with major health problems – terminal diseases and cancer – to explore buried attitudes and memories using dreams as the key. I find that this helps cancer patients in particular to come to terms with what is going on so they can fight back, rather than give in.

Nearly all illness, nearly all problems in relating to other people, in getting on with one's life, in dealing with one's work, will relate back to childhood. This is true in almost 99 per cent of cases. Even if your childhood has been relatively secure and happy, there is usually something that happened which makes you hold back on yourself and not trust yourself enough. Dreams can help you access and explain that memory.

What I do in my work is to teach people, on some levels, to 'play' with the unconscious so that you involve more of your consciousness, more of your brain capacity, and are able to get in touch with the part of you that *knows* what is happening.

Lack of Self Worth

One of my youthful dreams came out of my hatred for myself and my body: compared to everyone else I felt inadequate and useless. At eighteen or nineteen I began to understand that I was not unique in this attitude, and I know now that this problem of self-deprecation cripples half of humanity.

In my search for the cause of my lack of self-worth I had the following dream. I was in a college or university amongst groups of people who, with the aid of professors, were designing life plans, like blueprints for a building or scripts for a play. I saw how each person was helped to choose, not only his parents and friends, but also a particular mental, physical and emotional body, just as an actor is costumed for a part in a play. There was a sense of excitement and bustle. A voice said suddenly: 'It's time to get ready!' Everyone put on the bodies they had chosen.

But as they experienced the effect of what they had created, the atmosphere changed dramatically. Sighs and groans filled the air. No one remembered that these bodies were the tools they had chosen to help them learn what they themselves had decided to learn. 'It's not fair. I'm being punished,' some cried. 'It's too difficult – too painful!'

I then saw myself as one of them, and felt enormous pain. 'I can't cope!' I thought. 'What I've chosen is too much!' Now I realized where some of my inadequacy might come from.

The dream then showed me how the attitude of the mother and father to each other at the moment of conception, combined with the mother's response to knowing she was pregnant, also affected each person's self-worth. If those moments have involved pain or rejection we unconsciously identify with them and subsequently reject ourselves.

At the close of the dream I saw myself talking to groups of people about the importance of conception, pregnancy and birth. The idea that we choose a certain pattern in life is common to a number of spiritual and philosophical teachings. Many therapies today, such as rebirthing, have discovered the need to release birth and pre-birth trauma.

Much of my own work involves helping clients to remember, through dreams, counselling and deep relaxation techniques, to reconnect to memories that cause a hiccup in their ability to cope easily with life. By unlocking these memories, and by re-experiencing them, we can understand where some of the negative patterns in our behaviour and personality originate. We can then transform their power to trip us up into a positive energy that frees us to live fully and without fear, instead of merely trying to survive.

Lack of self-worth is the prime saboteur of human happiness in the world today. It is the Fisher King wound which results in dysfunctional people who, at best, never realize their full potential, and, at worst, become addicted to alcohol, drugs, gambling, excitement and escape.

Passive child abuse

Most of us come from abused backgrounds, though not necessarily physically or sexually. Instead we are passively abused, and thus emotionally crippled. Passive abuse is what a parent did not give or do to support the child. It includes lack of love, care and encouragement; also disapproval (both verbal and non-verbal), ridicule, intolerance, impatience and criticism. However, the most damaging and most common form of passive abuse is not 'being there' for a child.

A woman who keeps a spotless house, prepares the food, washes and irons the clothes – who is in effect 'a good mother', but who silently blames her family for putting her in this servile position and who lacks joy in all she does – is 'not there' for her children. She is a model for 'This is what it's like to be a woman, and it's totally unsatisfactory.' As a result her children, both boys and girls, learn not to trust their own anima or femaleness, thus denying the value of receptivity, feeling and understanding.

A girl who decides not to be like her mother often becomes more like that parent later in life, whereas a boy will frequently marry, or relate to, women who are not truly 'there' for him. There will be a dysfunction on some level – such as a communications problem, sexual incompatibility or a lack of emotional support and nurturing. A man who works hard all day, comes home, reads the paper, eats, watches TV and then goes to bed is 'not there' for his children or his wife.

This sows seeds of mistrust in the male or animus energy which we use to do everything in life: it is active, assertive, outgoing. If we do not trust it we tend to become either extremely hard-working, compulsive perfectionists in an attempt to compensate for our insecurity and inadequacy, or 'start-stoppers' – people who never complete what they start, or who have marvellous ideas but can never carry them out. A girl from this background usually partners a man, or a series of men, who are physically, mentally or emotionally detached.

In fact most relationships between couples consist of two half-people leaning on each others' projections, instead of two individuals, each complete in his or her own personality, who together create a greater wholeness. Most of us love personalities who represent what was not there during our childhood. We project an ideal of what these personalities should be like, and blame them when they fail to match up to it. The men and women closest to us reflect the health of our own inner male and female, so rather than blame others for the way they are we should try to discover what in us is creating this particular mirror image.

Our relationship with ourselves

Of course the prime relationship from which all others develop is the relationship with oneself, which I believe is the most important in our entire life. Even my relationship with God comes out of the one I have with myself. If my relationship with myself is judging, condemning and punitive, for me God will be a judging, punishing authority figure who will always find me wanting.

My acceptance or rejection of myself develops from how my parents related to each other and to me. My subsequent relationship with my peer group, both as child and as adult, will form from what was missing for me as a child. For example, maybe I needed approval and never got it. I will therefore seek it from others by giving to them in a way that usually denies my own needs and wants. The healing professions are full of people who unconsciously feed on the approval of those in their care. Similarly, I will later take out on children – mine, or those of others – what I find is not working to my satisfaction with my peers. And so the vicious circle perpetuates itself.

The Child Within

Most of us have a 'lost child' buried somewhere inside us, who needs as much love and care as any other child. One of the first steps in healing this child is to make contact with it and accept it exactly as it is. In fact, if we could treat all children by saying, 'I love you, even if I don't always like what you do', instead of 'You rotten, beastly, awful child, look what you've done!' we would separate who the child is from what he does, and generate a completely different attitude in the child to his self.

Seeking the attention we crave

People who hate or dislike themselves are unhappy people who will unconsciously (and sometimes even consciously!) make others unhappy. People who have no sense of worth may criticize, blame, steal and in general behave destructively, especially towards themselves. Sometimes to behave badly is the only way we know to get attention. Unfortunately, children get more attention when they are naughty and difficult than when they are playing happily. This sows seeds in our subconscious of 'I matter more when I'm crying, angry, in pain and suffering than when I'm happy.' In the future these seeds can flower and we can become sick (or develop other attention-getting behaviour) so that we can unconsciously claim the love and attention we need.

Most of us think that hate is the opposite of love. It is not. We have to care to hate. There is an energy in it, a dynamic, just as there is in love. The opposite of love is indifference. Because we all need love we will do anything rather than be ignored. If we could begin to affirm children's 'good' behaviour and ignore the 'bad', we would sow seeds of 'I matter more when I'm healthy, happy, joyous.' What a difference that would make!

A friend of mine, the youngest of five, grew up in an isolated part of Canada with few material possessions. She told me that when she or her brothers or sisters became ill or behaved badly they were sent to the top of the house and ignored. She remembers once lying in bed with a temperature of 105 degrees, feeling very ill and sorry for herself. No one came with hot water bottles, warm drinks or soothing hands. 'By lunchtime,' she said, 'even though I felt ill, I was bored. I could hear noise and laughter downstairs, so I got out of bed to join in.' As a result, she told me, none of the children was ever seriously ill. They are all now well into their sixties and seventies, and have had happy and abundant lives. It paid them to invest their energy in positive attitudes and good health, rather than in misery and depression.

My friend told me this story many years ago because she saw that I was investing so much of my own time and energy into caring for sick people that they actually enjoyed being ill. Without knowing it, I was helping them to stay unhealthy. Of course I am not suggesting that we ignore very sick children and put them in freezing cold attics when they have double pneumonia. But what I am suggesting is that if we could emphasize from a very early age the benefits of enjoying life, instead of reinforcing the negative in human behaviour, the world would be full of happier people. This attitude is very different from passive abuse or deliberate neglect; it is consciously helping the child to develop his fullest potential for life and happiness.

A dream that shocked me into realizing how badly I was treating myself and how sick my own inner child was came in response to a specific question that I wrote down before I went to sleep. In my dream I was strolling through a vast nursery which seemed suspended in space and stretched to infinity. I saw hundreds and hundreds of cots – a vast sea of cots filled with babies – and, to my amazement, only one nursemaid to look after them. Aghast at the impossibility of her task, I opened my mouth to speak; but suddenly my eye was caught by the most miserable baby I had ever seen. It lay on the base of the cot, which was made of iron and had no mattress or covering. I stared down at its tiny, stick-like arms and swollen belly covered with bruises and dirt, its running nose and oozing eyes. 'How *can* you let this baby get into such an appalling condition?' I demanded, quivering with indignation.

The nursemaid looked at me for a long moment before replying with great firmness: 'This is your baby.' A bolt of pain exploded in my stomach and I recognized the truth of what she had said. Instantly awake, I reviewed my life and thought about how I could heal this baby by changing the way I treated myself.

After some time I dozed off into a semi-sleep and saw a great ball of light balanced in the night sky. Suddenly this light erupted in a massive explosion, scattering tiny sparks of itself far and wide into the dark. There was a sense of enormous energy and excitement, which began to fade as the small sparks flew further and further away from their source and appeared to shrink in the engulfing darkness. I then saw these sparks of scattered light falling to earth like raindrops and incarnating into human beings. A voice said: 'One of the deepest and most primeval fears carried in the unconscious of many people is the fear that they do not exist. It comes from this original separation from the light.'

Again instantly awake, I wrote down these words and the dream. As I did so I realized that, if we were once one with this light, to be pushed out from it unexpectedly would be like being kicked out of home by our parents before we felt ready. We would almost feel guilty, as if we had done something wrong. I understood where another level of my own lack of self-worth might have come from, why I sometimes felt I was born guilty – aside from my karma, conception, birth, childhood and general life pattern.

I began to think about how we react when we feel ignored or left out. We feel hurt or irritated, and want to lash out. 'I'll show X. He can't ignore me like that!' Maybe we get angry and upset because when others treat us as if we don't exist it evokes this old primeval fear. We lash out, and unconsciously want to do something that says: 'See, I *do* exist. I matter. I'm important.' I realized that if we could treat one another with love and care, as if we were important and mattered even though we might never see one another again from that moment on, we would begin to heal that wound. I also saw that we must treat ourselves in the same way.

Returning to the Light

Fear, anger, disbelief in self love and the problems that arise from the lack of it, all merit a book of their own. However, dreams, visualization techniques and an active imagination are wonderful tools for discovering and healing many of these hurt, hidden and often despised parts of ourselves.

If someone comes to me with a problem, I always suggest that they invoke or ask for a dream to shed light on what happened in their past. Ask your dreams 'What am I meant to be learning from this?' 'How else can I learn this lesson?' 'Is there another way?'

I then ask them to write the dream down and tell me about it. Even if the dream doesn't tell the exact story, I get the person to pick out the key elements, those that strike a chord. Then I ask them to create a symbol or mandala with some of those elements in it and imagine that they are inside the symbol or inside aspects of the dream.

I ask them how old they are at this time, the time that the

problem really started. (It is important that this is answered intuitively, not rationally.) Then I ask them to go back to that age and go into what happened. What else was going on in their lives? How did they relate to their mother or father? What did they feel about life? If we think about our life as being like a movie, how would they *re*create the situation? I ask them to *imagine* how it might have been if that time had been different. *Imagine* hugging the person or child you were, playing with them, telling them you love them. *Imagine* hugging and loving and merging into one.

By discovering your lost child, your inner child, you will reconnect and remember. You will also release a lot of negative energy that has been held in for a long time. I do this exercise in a workshop to help heal fear, anger and lack of self-confidence.

You can use dreams to give extra insight into all aspects of your life. Even if someone doesn't remember a dream I'll ask them what colour it was. It's a doorway into the unconscious. You can work with anything. And once you have identified your lost bits and pieces – good and bad – you will begin to become whole again.

Gestalt – being each part of the dream (see page 74) – also gives people the opportunity to experience the feelings of different parts of themselves, parts that are often repressed or which they are completely unaware of. It allows the whole person to begin to speak.

Even if a dream doesn't seem to be specifically dealing with a particular problem – whether it is of the past, present or future – the very fact that a dream is happening now means that it is to do with now, and you can go through the 'now' into the past or future.

If only people knew how to get in touch with the source of a problem, they would discover how easily real healing can occur.

A Happy Childhood

We spend so much of our lives in sleep. Let's learn to use sleep productively as a time for healing, a time to change the things we don't like about ourselves. It is never too late to find our lost child, and dreams are one way to help us recreate our childhood in a way that is happy, carefree and healing.

4

SLEEP:
AN ALTERED STATE
OF CONSCIOUSNESS

In all of us, even in good men, there is a lawless wild beast
nature which peers out in sleep.

PLATO, *REPUBLIC*

The Phenomenon of Sleep

For many centuries sleep, dreams and altered states of consciousness have been a source of fascination for mankind. Some ancient civilizations thought sleep was a magical condition in which the soul left the body to commune with the gods. Artists, writers and musicians have used the phenomenon of sleep for inspiration and creativity. Men of science and philosophy speculated on the purpose of sleep and what happened to the brain during it, while men of religion believed that sleep was given by God as a divine blessing, a sign of love. In 1758 Samuel Johnson wrote:

Sleep is a state in which a great part of every life is passed.
No animal has been yet discovered, whose existence is not
varied with intervals of insensibility, and some late philo-
sophers have extended the empire of sleep over the veg-
etable world. Yet of this change so frequent, so great, so
general and so necessary, no searcher has yet found either
the efficient or final cause, or can tell by what power the
mind and body are thus chained down in irresistible stu-

pefaction, or what benefits the animal receives from this
alternate suspension of its active powers.

Since Dr Johnson's time, thanks to modern sleep research
laboratories we know a lot more about sleep than was known
then – although we still do not know everything. Initial
researches in the nineteenth century suggested that during the
day poisonous substances were formed in the body which were
only eliminated during sleep. Other theories were that sleep was
caused by the action of certain glands, upheavals in the circulation of the blood through the brain or muscular relaxation;
alternatively, even the lack of 'external stimuli' – in other words,
just plain boredom – could induce sleep.

It was gradually realized that, once sleep began, physiological
changes took place as a result of which the brain, heart, lungs
and nervous system slowed down and the digestive organs
became less active. At the same time questions were asked about
the mind and consciousness. What happened to the mind during
sleep, and where did consciousness go when sleep took over?

A source of spiritual nourishment

Earlier schools of philosophy and religion from the time of the
Chaldeans, Babylonians, ancient Egyptians and Greeks –
esoteric schools of initiation known as mystery schools – taught
that in sleep the spirit withdrew from the body to receive
spiritual nourishment. Initiates learned to invoke dreams in
which they sat at the feet of great teachers in universities called
the halls of wisdom and learning. While asleep, they visited
temples dedicated to healing and beauty and experimented with
the effects of vibration, water, touch, sound and crystals on the
physical, etheric, mental and emotional bodies. Students were
shown how to project their astral bodies (in other words, their
emotional bodies, which look like an ethereal counterpart of the
physical body) into other dimensions, how to read the Akasia
(the archetypal record of everything that has ever happened),
and how to assist souls at birth and death.

Sleep was a time of creativity and spiritual development. To use it as a form of escape, as many of us do today, was unheard of. During the day – day school – the soul slept, and lessons were learnt from what went on in daily life. At night – night school – the body slept, and the lessons came from within.

Esoteric schools taught students that in sleep and death consciousness was withdrawn rather than extinguished, so they should have no fear of dying. Astrology also played a significant part in the curriculum, and it was believed that the position of the planets at a person's birth, as well as the phases of the moon, had a decisive effect on the pattern of that person's sleep at night. When the moon is full I find it very hard to sleep, and even during the day I feel a bit hyped up. Because sleep appeared to approximate the state of consciousness reached through contemplation or meditation, many exercises evolved to still the mind and induce a sleep-like state without loss of awareness. This state was used both on its own, to teach relaxation of the body while controlling the mind, and as a preparation for sleep, which was considered a sacred rite.

Preparation for sleep

Communities such as the Essenes, to which Joseph and Mary, the parents of Jesus, belonged believed that preparation for sleep was as important as preparation for death. In fact to the Essenes sleep was a little death and they went to bed in the calm acceptance that they might not wake up the next morning. This was not morbid. It meant rather that the Essenes greeted each day like a new birth, a new life, unique and valuable, and at the end of it nothing was left undone. Before the sun went down arguments, disagreements and quarrels were settled. The day was reviewed, accepted, forgiven and released. Like the Senoi of Malaysia, the Essenes were reputed to be completely balanced psychologically because, both in and out of their dreams, they fearlessly faced whatever lay in their path.

The Essenes went to sleep knowing that they were part of God's consciousness, giving thanks for the day and aligning themselves with the possibility of what tomorrow might bring. They worked hard, ate simple food, bathed daily in water, air and the sun's rays, and attuned to the angelic forces of each day according to the Essene tree of life. Their daily disciplines, as described in the Dead Sea Scrolls, amounted to practical common sense and brought peace to body, mind and spirit. The Essene philosophy of sleep is virtually identical to that of the famous dream interpreter Edgar Cayce, who was active in the 1920s and 1930s. Cayce said:

Sleep is the period when the soul takes stock of what it has acted upon from one rest period to another; drawing comparisons, as it were, that make for harmony, peace, joy, love, long-suffering, patience, brotherly love and kindness – all fruits of the spirit. Hate, harsh words, unkind thoughts and oppression are fruits of Satan. The soul either abhors what it has passed through, or it enters into the joy of the Lord.

Altered states

Sleep, it seems, is therefore a time of purging, healing, physical relaxation and psychological adjustment. Edgar Cayce's words match descriptions of the type of assessment experienced by numerous near-death survivors and suggest that in sleep we may have experiences similar to those at and after death.

The Tibetan Book of the Dead graphically describes the images of fear, horror, threat or punishment we may see after death, but stresses that these are self-created thought forms based on our beliefs. Tibetan lamas are trained to keep a dying person conscious as long as possible, in order to guide him past these illusions as they arise. For the days preceding, during and after death the patient will be reminded to keep moving towards the light, to face any threatening figure but not to become emotionally involved with it, to remember that it is a figment of his imagination. Tibetan dream yoga is a form of dress rehearsal for mastering the challenges of this experience. As in the ancient mystery schools, a student learns to retain consciousness throughout the night, while in a sleep-like state. He controls what is going on around him in his inner world, and is therefore ready to do the same at death.

After an accident, in which the car I was driving was hit by an overtaking truck and smashed to bits, I had a dream in which I saw six lords of karma standing in front of me, awesome and tall. I felt my knees tremble. The first pointed to a body that appeared miraculously beside me and stood empty but erect, like a suit of armour. I got into it and performed, like a mime artist, until the second lord pointed to another body, which I had to get into also. I did this six times until a voice said: 'You chose to live twelve lives in one. You have now completed six.' As I looked at these stern judging figures before me I suddenly realized that they were aspects of me and that I was judging myself. At once, we all fell about with laughter. It was as if they had been on stilts, and the stilts had collapsed. I awoke, absolutely sure that for me God is a God of love and humour, and that if we choose to believe in punishment and judgement we administer it to ourselves.

Sleep as a route to understanding others

Parapsychological research into the nature of consciousness suggests that during sleep there is greater telepathic rapport with others. We 'let go' our ego boundaries and become more open, more receptive to people known and unknown around us. The physicist Albert Einstein wrote about the need to free ourselves from the prison of feeling that we were separate from everyone else by widening our circle of compassion to embrace all living creatures. It seems that in sleep we can all do this. The closer we are to one another, the more empathy we feel, so the greater the likelihood of telepathic and clairvoyant 'tuning in'. Husbands and wives, friends and lovers can not only develop identical sleeping patterns, but can also often dream the same dreams at the same time. To blend with another in sleep is charming; however, it can also be a powerful resource for dealing with the problems of waking life.

I once spent four weeks travelling with a group of twenty-five people who bickered and quarrelled their way around Europe. It was my unfortunate responsibility to organize the bedroom arrangements and each night I was faced with a queue of people saying: 'I don't want to sleep with X because he or she smokes/ snores/ gets up at 2 a.m./ spends too much time in the bathroom/ never stops talking/ never talks at all/ doesn't like me', and so on. On one occasion we arrived after midnight at a hotel which made a mistake with our booking, so they offered us two big rooms with mattresses on the floor. We all piled in, regardless of gender, propensity to snore or anything else. We had to be up at 5 a.m. to catch a bus and, in spite of there being only two bathrooms, everyone was ready, bright and good-tempered. From that moment the bickering about who should sleep where stopped: it was as if overnight all our rough edges had smoothed out and melded together.

Sleeping in the same room as others is another route to insight and understanding. A group of businessmen, whose company was fraught with business and personality problems which official meetings had not solved, read a newspaper article suggesting that 'to sleep together was to meet together'. So they decided to go away for a camping weekend, taking one big tent in which all of them would sleep. They knew nothing about dreams or dream incubation (see Chapter 7). That weekend they lolled about, hardly discussed anything pertaining to business, slept more than ate, and, without having experienced any magical dream or received any deep insight, returned home.

However, on some unconscious level a blending had occurred. The following week each man produced an idea that on its own was not practical, but which, when put together with the ideas of the others, developed into a venture that was successfully carried out. Since then they have used the 'sleep on it together' technique many times, and the company is now thriving.

A clinical psychologist friend, Sylvia, took a job in an American hospital that she soon discovered was known for the violence of its inmates as well as for the drug, straitjacket and padded-cell treatment they received. After her first day she wanted to leave, and that night fell into an exhausted, nerve-racked sleep in which her mind became a pulsing web of light that kept expanding until it seemed to contain the entire hospital. She saw every floor, corridor and ward, while the faces of inmates rose and fell around her.

Then Sylvia seemed to be floating out of her body to the top floor of the hospital, where she had not yet been. There were a series of padlocked doors, but she floated through them into wards where the patients appeared to be in wired-off compartments like cages. When they saw her they floated towards her, crying out and calling for help. She did not know how to help, but she greeted each one, took a hand, stroked a face, told them her name and promised to return.

When she awoke she remembered nothing of this, but plunged into her work with new vigour and felt a different rapport with the staff. In the afternoon the matron said she wanted to introduce her to patients and staff as yet unmet. They went to the top floor of the hospital, and suddenly Sylvia recognized the corridors and padlocked doors of her previous night's experience. The matron told her it was too dangerous to go inside the ward without two male nurse 'guards', because these were the most violent and crazy of the hospital's inmates, but that she could look through the glass panels.

Sylvia, however, insisted on going inside, and as she did so every patient stood up, saying: 'Sylvie, Sylvie, you've come back!' She felt shivers run down her spine as she greeted each patient exactly as she had done in her dream. In some way her consciousness had blended with her patients' – it was not one-way, but mutual. They recognized and knew her.

Before she arrived, psychologists would only enter these wards with a guard. Sylvia, who always went in alone, was never harmed, and spent the next twenty years working to rehabilitate these people. When she needed to develop a deeper understanding with a particular person or group, she slept in the hospital with them; not in the same room, but as close as possible. Sleep for Sylvia was as productive as anything she did during her waking hours, and enabled her to respond intuitively to the temperament of everyone around her. (It is not always possible to sleep with everyone with whom we want good rapport! I find, however, that writing a name on a piece of paper and sleeping on it can produce similar results. It is as if by doing this we 'call' the other person into our orbit.)

Edgar Cayce

Probably the most productive sleeper of all time was Edgar Cayce, who was frequently called 'The sleeping prophet'. Even as a child he slept on his school books, and overnight absorbed the information that they contained. When awake he was able to recite fluently what he had learnt in his sleep. As a young man Cayce was selling encyclopedias – a job he hated – when his vocal cords became paralysed and he lost his voice. After all orthodox treatment failed his family took him to a hypnotist at a local fair, who put him into a deep sleep or trance state in which Cayce diagnosed the cause and recommended the cure for his own condition. He later learnt to induce for himself this state, which bypassed the conscious mind and gave access to what he called the wisdom of the subconscious and what Jung called the collective unconscious. He needed only the name and geographical location of anyone anywhere in the world to give a detailed diagnosis of that person's condition.

During his life he helped thousands of people, and since his death in 1945 his readings, carefully documented by the Association of Research and Enlightenment in Virginia Beach, have helped thousands more. Cayce's life and work have been the subject of dozens of books. He is still the most extraordinary example of how we can use sleep to delve into the unconscious, although he always insisted that anyone who was willing to develop his psychic and spiritual faculties could do the same.

The wild beast in all of us

Delving into our own hidden depths may not always, of course, be entirely without its perils. Plato talks about the 'wild beast nature which peers out in sleep', and psychologists say that in sleep we face aspects of submerged personality which could well be our own wild beast nature or shadow side. The French philosopher Descartes may well have been agreeing with Plato when he wrote: 'I am accustomed to sleep, and in my dreams to imagine the same things that lunatics imagine when awake.' Even the psychologist William James said, when discussing sleep, that it would be 'a dreadful disease, but for its familiarity'.

Freud, however, suggested that 'Sleep is an act which reproduces intra-uterine existence, fulfilling the conditions of repose, warmth and absence of stimulus; indeed, in sleep many people resume a foetal position.' For most of us, sleep brings balance, peace and renewal. Without it, we become disjointed, angry and dysfunctional. In experiments with rats, sleep deprivation has actually caused death. Most of us spend approximately six to eight hours asleep daily, and Edgar Cayce readings (see pp. 21–22) indicate that seven and a half to eight hours a day are what most bodies need to recuperate. ('Most bodies' refers not just to people, but also to the physical, mental, emotional and spiritual bodies.)

The different states of sleep

The various types of brainwave rhythm are referred to by letters of the Greek alphabet. When we make the decision to go to sleep our brainwave rhythm is in Beta. This is the active, assessing, decision-making part of the brain, which we use all day. As our muscles relax and we drift into a half-asleep, half-awake state we lower this rhythm into Alpha, which is slower and more receptive. Listening to music, watching a movie or television, daydreaming, deep breathing, creative visualization – any kind of deep relaxation puts us into Alpha. The closer we are to sleep, the deeper the Alpha state we sink into, and when we finally sleep and dream our brainwave rhythm moves into Theta, which is slower still. Delta, the slowest rhythm of all, usually only occurs when we are so profoundly asleep that we are unconscious, as when we are fully anaesthetized or a foetus in the womb. There are people, such as yogis in India, who can induce Delta as a form of spiritual discipline, and put themselves into a near-death trance in which they themselves control their own respiration and circulation, instead of these being automatic reflex actions.

It is when we are in the half-asleep, half-awake Alpha phase, which occurs both when we fall asleep and when we come out of it, that hypnagogic images appear. These are normally very clear, and can include faces (sometimes our own), trees, shrubs, animals, landscapes, dots, spots, stars – there is in fact no limit to what might arise before us when our brains begin to relax. In 1861 Alfred Maury, a French scientist, published a book in which he described his own experiments with 'hypnagogic hallucinations'. He discovered he could trigger all sorts of visions, in which people even appeared to speak to him, by pressing on his own eyeballs. Maury was also fascinated by the effect on the brain of external stimuli applied to the body during sleep. In experiments on himself while he was asleep, he got friends to shine a light on his eyelids, tickle him with a feather, apply cold or heat, and drip water on various parts of his body. Each time his brain responded by creating scenes that incorporated the physical sensation.

Research into the relationship between body, mind, brain, sleep and consciousness began hundreds of years ago, although it was not until the physics of electricity was understood that instruments for measuring the brain and nervous system developed. Long before this, Aristotle speculated that the mind was located in the heart, while in the second century AD Galen, the Roman physician, conducted experiments with Barbary apes in which he caused them to become unconscious by squeezing their brains, and as a result decided that the mind was sited in the brain. Galen also discovered that the brain controls the voice, and so concluded that the brain was the organic seat of consciousness and that the soul was attached to the brain.

Over the centuries, anatomical study of the brain led to analysis of the nervous system and the supposition that the brain was most probably the source of consciousness, and therefore controlled the changes of consciousness that occur in sleep. Allan Hobson, the psychiatrist and neuroscientist who wrote in the 1980s *The Dreaming Brain*, says: 'Consciousness is the continuous subjective awareness of the activity of billions of cells firing at many times a second, communicating instantaneously with tens of thousands of its neighbours.' He adds: 'And the organization of this symphony of activity is such that it is sometimes externally oriented (during waking), sometimes oblivious to the external world (during sleep), and sometimes so remarkably aware of itself (during dreams) that it recreates the external world in its own image.'

Both Freud and his contemporary, Santiago Ramón y Cajal, the founder of modern neurobiology, studied the brain in the belief that it was the physical foundation of the mind. Even when Freud abandoned neurobiology it continued to shape his dream and psychoanalytical work. He assumed, however, that the nervous system was stimulated from outside, whereas current brain research shows that it generates its own energy, is not dependent on external information to function, and has a dynamic internal life of its own with which it can interact with the outside world.

The brain is an incredibly complex information machine which scientists, physicians and neurobiologists view from one point of view, and psychiatrists and psychologists from another. With the invention of EEG (electroencephalogram) instruments, which amplify brain voltage, scientists really began to understand how the brain works. In 1952 EEGs enabled two researchers named Kleitman and Aserinsky to make a breakthrough in sleep research which connected rapid eye movement to dreaming, and paved the way for a new phase of sleeping-brain investigation.

REM discoveries

Nathaniel Kleitman was a physiologist and sleep scientist at the University of Chicago. In 1939 he wrote a book describing the physiology of sleep based on his work with a French physiologist, Henri Pieron, in Paris. Eugene Aserinsky was a graduate student working in Kleitman's laboratory.

Aserinsky was interested in the attention span of children, and noticed that when they lost focus their eyes closed and they fell into a light sleep. He decided to record both brainwave rhythm and eyelid movement when this happened. The results showed brain activity and rapid eye movements. Kleitman suspected that this might be connected to dreaming, and he and Aserinsky began to experiment, first with Aserinsky's son Armond, then with other volunteers.

They discovered that during sleep the brain had periods of activity as intense as when its owner was awake, which demolished the theory that the sleeping brain was resting. These episodes were connected to REM (rapid eye movement), which appeared to be associated with dreaming. They monitored REM asleep and non-REM sleep throughout the night, and found that when a person was woken up during REM he had not only been dreaming but could also remember the dream in vivid detail. In fact, 80 per cent of sleepers woken up *after* REM remembered dreaming, while if they were woken *during* the full burst of REM the figure rose to 95 per cent. Sleepers left to sleep without interruptions usually remembered no dreams.

REM sleep was found to occur in all mammals except the spiny anteater and, to a limited extent, in birds and reptiles. We have almost all seen the rapid eye movements and twitching paws of cats and dogs when they sleep and dream. A new-born baby spends eight hours a day in REM sleep, and before birth, thirty weeks after conception, the developing child appears to spend almost all its time in REM sleep. Children aged three to seven, monitored in a sleep laboratory, rarely reported dreams, whereas after the age of seven they dreamed as much as adults. In my own, non-laboratory, dream work with children aged five, six and seven, I found they all had dreams which they could describe quite graphically. If children are encouraged to share dreams from the moment they can talk, as in the Senoi culture, they will generally dream and remember the dream.

While living in America I worked briefly with Dr Stanley Krippener, a psychologist specializing in dream therapy and research. When watching him at work I saw that a sleeper, after three days of being woken up four or five times in mid-REM sleep, became confused and emotional. After seven days of being subjected to this treatment, the sleeper became irrational and unbalanced. When woken up continuously during non-REM sleep he was tired but not unduly upset. I realized that it is not sleep but dream deprivation that is so harmful. Dreams keep us emotionally balanced and healthy; without them we would become hallucinating psychotics.

Jenny, a young girl working as a ship's cook off northern

Australia, told me that when the prawns were running the entire crew had to help haul in the nets, no matter what their 'official' job was. This meant that approximately every three hours, night and day, a whistle blew to call all hands on deck. She said that after a few days it was frightening to witness the disintegration of the people round her. Jenny herself felt vulnerable, weepy and homesick, but many of the men erupted into violence and began to fight. Finally one man attacked another with a knife and killed him.

Jenny told me this story while attending a dream workshop in which she heard me speak about dreams and health. She said that many of the crew began to hallucinate after continuously interrupted sleep, but connected it to lack of sleep rather than lack of dreams. Of course lack of sleep can make us feel tired, irritated and disoriented, but lack of dreams affects us more profoundly.

One of the simplest but most effective methods of torture – which psychologically reduces the subject to a gibbering idiot while leaving no physical marks – is to wake him every hour night and day. No one should ever underestimate the importance of sleep. There is a supposition that primitive man, in order to survive, slept lightly and awoke at frequent intervals, his body charged with adrenalin, ready for fight or flight. Evolution brought changes, and man began to sleep longer, but his brain still moved in cycles of slow-wave deep sleep and lighter, more brain-active, sleep. The adrenalin and/or chemicals that were once used to wake him for immediate action were now used to stimulate inner action in the form of dreams. If this sleeping process is constantly interrupted we hallucinate, lose touch with reality and behave like someone who has taken a drug overdose. If the adrenalin 'cycle of arousal' theory is true, then the constantly interrupted sleeper is overburdened with a mass of self-generated chemical energy that has not been released through dreams. This chemical imbalance appears to blur the barrier between conscious and unconscious, so that our perception of the world around us is diminished.

Research shows that during REM sleep there are brain cells that turn on while others turn off. The cells that turn off release neurotransmitters, chemicals that are crucial to attention, learning and memory – maybe this is why so many of us forget our dreams! REM sleep begins about ninety minutes after we fall asleep. At the same time the brain speeds up, blood pressure rises, breathing quickens and the heart beats faster. Despite the fact that our muscles are relaxing we may twitch, or even mutter and sigh under our breath. We are in another world, a self-created universe. Episodes of REM dreams – which occur every ninety minutes, four to five times a night – are separated by periods of calmer, deeper, non-REM or slow-wave sleep. Non-REM shows brain activity, but statistically less dreaming. We spend approximately two hours, or 25 per cent, of each night in REM; according to research, this adds up to six years in an average lifetime. In these six years the brain-mind is brilliantly creative – yet this is time which most of us throw away, because we ignore our dreams instead of using them to enhance our lives.

5

THE GREAT
DREAM INTERPRETERS

Sigmund Freud

There have been many dream pioneers down the centuries, but it is thanks to Freud and his experiments early in the present century that we have learned to take dreams seriously. Since the discovery of REM some of his theories have been called into question, but it was Freud's work that laid the foundation for serious dream study.

As a doctor and neurologist, Freud had patients with symptoms of physical disease but who appeared, on further examination, to have nothing wrong organically. Because of this he became frustrated with straight clinical practice and, with a Viennese colleague, Dr Joseph Breuer, began to experiment with what were then unorthodox ideas. After using hypnosis, they decided that their patients were suffering from persistent painful memories which affected their attitudes and behaviour. Freud recognized many phobias as being defences against unbearable feelings which were repressed, and could only come out in the form of physical or mental symptoms. He found that, if he let his patients talk freely, not only did they lead him to the original core of their neuroses but they also talked about their dreams – and the dreams in turn led to new ideas and memories. Freud realized that dreams revealed hidden emotional conflicts that caused mental and physical disorder. So he abandoned conventional medicine and reverted to what many of his colleagues thought smacked of superstition and the occult – the study of dreams.

A forerunner in the ancient world

Long before this a Roman soothsayer, Artemidorus of Ephesus, wrote a book on dreams and their interpretation which had a profound effect on all subsequent dream research. Artemidorus drew on both the Egyptian and Greek civilizations for the material for his book, the *Oneirocritica*, and, like them, believed that 'dreams and visions are infused into men for their advantage and instruction'. Hundreds of years later, Edgar Cayce said almost the same thing: 'All dreams are given for the benefit of the dreamer', but he added: 'would that he interpret them correctly'.

Even though in Artemidorus' time – the second century AD – dreams were still believed to come from the gods and were the province of soothsayers, clairvoyants and psychics rather than of priests and healers, Artemidorus himself realized that he could not be too arbitrary or oversimplify when he interpreted a dream. He said: 'The rules of dreaming are not general and therefore cannot satisfy all persons, but often, according to times and persons, they admit of "varied interpretation".' He pointed out that a man may dream good and bad dreams in one night, as well as good and bad things in one dream. In analysing a dream Artemidorus also took into consideration the name and occupation of the dreamer, as well as the conditions under which the dream occurred. He was fascinated by the emotions that dreams evoked, and the difference between dreams arising out of everyday life and those that had a larger vision.

Artemidorus worked with what Freud later called 'free association' – bringing to mind whatever the dream image evoked. However, it was what the dream image meant to Artemidorus that mattered, instead of what it meant to the dreamer as was the case with Freud. Artemidorus encouraged dream incubation because he believed the gods could help us see more clearly 'what is going on in us'. He also wrote: '. . . but we should never ask the gods undue questions, and if the answer has been granted we must not forget to sacrifice and give thanks'.

Artemidorus' attitude to dreams was extraordinarily sophisti-
cated. Many of his suggestions are as applicable to us today as
they were to his fellow citizens nearly two thousand years ago,
and his *Oneirocritica* was used first by Freud and later by Jung,
both of whom paid tribute to his work.

Freud and the unconscious

In 1897 Sigmund Freud wrote to a friend: 'I have felt impelled to
start writing about dreams with which I feel on safe ground.' He
realized that he would have to study not only his own dreams but
also his own psyche. With ruthless honesty he probed his earliest
childhood memories and emotions, and found it extremely painful to lay bare 'the humble origins of much pride and precedence'.
The result of this intense self-examination was the basis for his
belief in the unconscious as the source of all motivation and
behaviour. Freud was one of the first to attempt to chart the
unconscious, and he paved the way for all future exploration.

He divided the psyche into the id, the ego and the superego.
The id is the primitive, instinctual part of us that, according to
Freud, dominates the unconscious. The superego is the sum total
of conscience and social conditioning, while the ego is our conscious self that mediates between the two. Freud's theory was
that during sleep the ego withdrew, which released the id to go
on the rampage. It did this by stirring up memories of unfulfilled
wishes and unacknowledged desires – most of them Oedipal
sexual urges – buried in the unconscious, which it then tried to
present to the ego through dreams.

Because these images might shock the ego and interrupt sleep,
what he called the censor part of the mind disguised them. Freud
called the disguise, or apparent meaning, the manifest content,
and the true, hidden, meaning the latent content. He believed
that most of man's conscious desires were so alien to his usual
personality that when they attempted to find expression through
his dreams the censor always tried to protect him by changing
them. For this reason Freud called dreams 'the guardians of
sleep' – the guardians of sanity too, if what lies buried in the
unconscious is so outrageous.

In addition to his work on the id, the ego and the superego, and his ideas on repressed libido and wish fulfilment, Freud also introduced the world to the Oedipus complex and the Freudian slip – the slip of the tongue that usually reveals a hidden and often unpalatable truth. The Oedipus complex – from the famous Greek legend of King Oedipus – is sexual desire by a child for the parent of the opposite sex. Freud believed that most people had hostile attitudes to one or both parents, usually to the parent of the same sex, as the desire came out of incestuous sexual rivalry.

Freud presented ideas which both shocked and stimulated his contemporaries, many of whom could not accept his reduction of nearly all symbols in dreams to a sexual interpretation. However, Freud was a true pioneer, and when he published his classic work *The Interpretation of Dreams* in 1900 he established for all time the importance of dreams in psychoanalysis and in life.

Carl Jung

At the same time that Freud's great work on dreams was exciting considerable interest in Europe another man, who was to become known as one of the world's greatest psychoanalysts and thinkers, became an assistant physician at the Burghölzli mental hospital in Zürich. Like Freud, Jung had been medically and neurologically trained, but, after reading a description of psychoses as 'diseases of the personality' in Krafft-Ebbing's *Textbook of Psychiatry*, had a flash of insight that psychiatry was the only possible area for him.

At the Burghölzli hospital word association tests were used as a means of studying the way in which the mind links similar or contrasting themes. Jung developed this as a tool for exploring an emotional preoccupation or 'hidden impulse', which he was later to describe as a complex. In spite of using word association to discover hidden complexes, Jung preferred not to use free association with dreams. With each element in the dream free-association, coined by Freud, led the dreamer back to the repressed or forgotten incident that was now causing emotion, neurosis or discomfort. Jung felt that this technique distorted the dream as a whole, and often led the dreamer away from the dream.

Dream symbolism

Jung believed that a dream stood on its own merits, and was a statement of profound authority on the dreamer's life because it was independent of conscious control. His attitude to dream interpretation was to question the purpose of the dream and discover why the unconscious chose a particular symbol, and what it was trying to show the dreamer about his life and his attitude to it. Unlike Freud, who said that certain symbols had general or universal meaning, Jung felt that symbols had a power unique to the dreamer and could not be confined to a narrow interpretation. An example is Jung's suggestion that a circle *may* be a symbol of wholeness, or integration of personality, whereas Freud classified anything resembling a circle or container as symbolizing female sexuality.

Jung treated the dreamer as the most important part of the dream, and adapted his methods to the individual needs of the patient. He stressed that unless the dream made sense to the dreamer there was no such thing as successful interpretation. Jung once said: 'If we meditate on a dream sufficiently long and thoroughly – if we take it about with us and turn it over and over – something almost always comes out of it.' He also thought that dreams were easier to understand in series than on their own. I have found this true of many of my own dreams when, over a period, certain themes recur, or a later dream comments on an earlier one and clarifies its meaning.

Collective unconscious

Jung's early hospital work with schizophrenic patients laid the foundation for much of his future psychoanalytical study. He saw that mental illness was characterized by a disunity or fragmentation of the personality, and his discovery that many delusions and hallucinations had similar themes – most of which paralleled worldwide religious and historical myths and legends – led him to formulate the idea of the collective unconscious. Some of his patients with no religious background dreamed of angels and devils, gods and goddesses, while others saw Beauty and the Beast-type heroes and heroines, Roman slaves, magicians, Aztec princesses, handsome crusaders and wise men. He later found the same universality of symbols in primitive tribes completely cut off from civilization by geographical location, culture and language, and saw that they corresponded to images in ancient myths, art and religion about which the dreamers could not possibly have known.

Jung realized that the collective unconscious was a level of mind where all men were one, and that it was impersonal, transpersonal and the source of all that evolves in the conscious mind. The writer and explorer Laurens van der Post, who knew Jung well, described the unconscious as 'a great area of unknown spirit and awareness in man which remains the same for all, regardless of race or creed. In all human beings there is such an area in which the whole of life participates, as it were, mystically.'

Archetypes

To Jung the collective unconscious contained the wisdom of the ages. He believed that the more attuned to it man was, through dreams, visions and active imagination, the more balanced, integrated and happy his life and personality would be. He defined the primordial universal images arising out of the unconscious as archetypes, based on Plato's ideal forms, or patterns in the divine mind that predetermine the formation of the material world. An archetype is an innate, spontaneously recurring pattern within the collective psyche of all mankind. Actors, actresses, politicians, public figures, heroes and heroines in books can become archetypal figures for us too. They symbolize certain character traits or behaviour patterns, as well as life, death, joy, conflict, war, peace, male, female, winner, loser. Archetypal figures can appear in our dreams in the form of the wise old man or woman, the warrior queen, the great mother, the young hero, the Holy Child and many others. This does not mean that *all* dream figures are archetypes; most of them are aspects of ourselves disguised as people we know.

Jung's work with dreams, archetypes and the collective unconscious had a worldwide influence on writers, scholars, artists, philosophers and psychologists. His theories affected the study of myths, religion and literature. Many Jungian terms, such as the complex, the persona, the shadow, synchronicity (clusters of significant events occurring together), animus and anima, the introvert and extrovert, and individuation (the process of becoming a separate indivisible unity or complete human being, whole but *not* separate from the human race), have now become almost household words.

The persona is the face we present to the world, the way we want others to see us, while the shadow is the opposite of the persona, the suppressed, unaccepted part we usually project onto others and sometimes see in our dreams. The shadow lives in what Jung called the personal unconscious, which contains specific individual experiences and characteristics, in contrast to the collective unconscious, which contains elements common to all mankind. Jung's *personal* unconscious inhabited by the shadow is similar to Freud's unconscious inhabited by the unruly id. Animus and anima (Latin for soul) are the inner masculine and feminine counterparts of man and woman. Jung felt these inner men and women were soul images connecting us to God.

Active imagination

For Jung psychology was the science of the soul, and he spent his entire life trying to help people to understand themselves. He thought that dreams were not only a vital part of the psyche's balancing system, but also a means of coming to terms with the whole of life. He believed that the unconscious offered guidance unobtainable from any other source, and he found that many of his mid-life crisis patients, who described feelings of isolation and emptiness, really suffered from separation from the rich, emotional life of the unconscious.

Most neuroses involve feelings of fragmentation or disassociation from other parts of the psyche. Jung concentrated on a patient's relationship with these split-off or sub-personality parts by using active imagination – a conscious discovery of, and dialogue with, what lives in the unconscious. It is similar to dreaming, but the subject is fully awake; the conscious mind participates, while in a dream it does not. Often these sub-personalities living in the unconscious have very different ideas from those of the conscious mind. Using the imagination as a meeting point can ultimately lead to their integration – which is part of the individuation process.

So fascinated was Jung by the personality that he once wrote: 'From my eleventh year I have been launched on a single enterprise, which is my "main business". My life has been permeated and held together by one idea and one goal – namely to penetrate the secret of the personality. Everything can be explained from this point, and all my works relate to this one theme.'

Freud and Jung: Different Approaches to Dreams

When Jung met Freud he already had very definite ideas about the powers of the unconscious, and felt that dreams were its natural expression. Although inspired by much of Freud's work, he could never accept that a dream was a 'facade behind which meaning lies hidden – a meaning already known but maliciously held, so to speak, from the consciousness'. He felt that, like all things in nature, the dream expressed itself as best it could, and any misunderstanding was due to an inner short-sightedness on the part of the dreamer, rather than deliberate deception on the part of the dream.

Freud thought that the majority of dreams had at their inner-most core unacceptable wishes based on incestuous fantasies from childhood; these fantasies, especially those from the first five years of a child's life, were also central to most adult neuroses. Jung agreed that it was valuable to look for possible childhood origins of neurosis, but believed it came mainly from the present, so that what Freud unearthed was of secondary importance. Jung also disagreed with Freud's assumption that all association led back to sex. There is a story that Jung once put this question to Freud in a lecture: if in a dream such things as a tower, a key, a knife, a sword, a stick, a tree, a pole all meant a penis, then what did a penis itself mean?

Freud's idea that the unconscious was a repository for everything shameful was completely alien to Jung's understanding of the unconscious as a guide and a friend. He believed in delving into the unconscious to search for gold, rather than to purge past sexual frustrations. Jung's attitude to the libido, which was very different from Freud's, finally cost him his friendship with his colleague. For Jung libido was not merely the force behind sexuality, but also the divine creative force of nature. After studying the archetypal roots of Oedipal situations, which were the cornerstone of Freud's sexual theories, Jung believed that incest should be understood symbolically and not literally – that it was a phase of evolution in the collective unconscious to a higher form of consciousness. Freud was unable to accept this divergence from the truths he believed he had discovered, and broke off his association with Jung.

Other Interpreters

In spite of their differences, the ideas of both Jung and Freud have had a profound effect on our own attitude to our dreams today, and their thinking has coloured the world of modern psychology. So too have the ideas of countless other researchers into dreams, including Alfred Maury, Hervey St Denis – who in

1867 wrote that 'the dream shows us the scaffolding of the mental apparatus, as one rarely perceives it in real life' – Arthur Schopenhauer, William Stekel, Alfred Adler, Mary Arnold-Forster, Havelock Ellis and many more. Alfred Maury, who was fascinated by hypnagogic hallucinations, and Hervey St Denis showed, by studying their own dreams and experimenting with controlled and lucid dreaming, that it was possible both to increase and to gain access to dreams simply by paying attention to them. Havelock Ellis, trying to find how the difference between the physical cause of dreams and their emotional content could be resolved, wrote that emotions welled up in dreams 'because the fetters of civilization are loosened and we know the fearful joy of freedom'. He believed that through dreams there was a way of synthesizing feelings, memories and physical sensations.

Calvin Hall

Most modern dream interpreters such as Calvin Hall, Fritz Perls, Eric Fromm and Arnold Mindell believe that dreams are not just the royal road to the unconscious, but a royal road to life itself. Calvin Hall, a psychologist and dream researcher, decided, like Abraham Maslow, founder of Humanistic and Transpersonal Psychology – study of the whole person beyond what is merely physical – that it was important to study the dreams of healthy people, and not just those of the sick. He wrote a book based on ten thousand dreams which he recorded and analysed in people's homes – rather than in hospitals or clinics – and in which he stressed that anyone capable of following simple instructions can interpret dreams. Like Jung, Hall preferred to analyse a collection of dreams rather than one on its own. He believed that with a hundred dreams from the same person he could accurately diagnose his or her personality. Hall's book, *The Meaning of Dreams*, suggests that he saw dreams as a complete reflection of what we think about ourselves and life, that dreams are 'pictures of the mind', and that if we can get meaning from a picture we can get meaning from a dream.

Fritz Perls

Calvin Hall and Fritz Perls both wanted to strip dream interpretation of its psychological mystique and make dreamwork easy and available for everyone. Perls originally trained as a Freudian analyst, but after a time preferred to use dreams as a route to integration rather than as a route to the past. He developed Gestalt therapy – the German word *gestalt* which means whole or complete. In dreamwork Gestalt therapy focuses on a person's body language, facial expression and voice while he retells the dream in the present, acts it out and thus re-experiences each part of the dream. Perls saw every image and symbol as an alienated part of the personality, and believed it was essential not only to discover them, but also to integrate them. In this way their energy became positive and helpful, rather than destructive.

Gestalt techniques, both in and out of dreams, include placing a chair or cushion opposite a person so that he can move back and forth when dialoguing with different parts of himself. In this way he totally identifies with each part. Perls, like Hall, looked at dreams as messages telling us where we were with ourselves and with life, and believed it was more important to bring this message to life by acting it out than by interpreting it.

An example of the power of bringing the dream or vision to life is the story of Black Elk, an American Indian who, during an almost fatal illness when he was nine years old, had a spectacular vision in which he saw four groups of twelve horses coming from the four corners of the world, each group a different colour. Suddenly one horse called out, and the air was filled with a storm of plunging, neighing horses as they took Black Elk up into the sky with them to meet the powers of the North, South, East and West, the Sky and the Earth in the form of six grandfathers – the ancestral spirits of his tribe who ruled the world. They each handed him a gift of power and healing, and showed him how he could use it to help his people, and through them the world.

When Black Elk recovered he was afraid to speak about his vision. While he was growing up it simmered inside him, but he still did nothing about it. When he was sixteen, Black Elk suddenly developed a fear of thunderstorms, hearing in the midst of them the voices of his vision calling him to make haste. When he finally spoke to the medicine man about this, he was told that his fear came from not sharing the vision, and that he must do so or something bad would happen.

The preparation for Black Elk to share his vision with his tribe was similar to that of a Vision Quest (see page 99). He had to fast, sweat and purify himself. The vision was then told, and later enacted through song and dance with members of the tribe playing the people and animals of the vision. The tribe felt better and many people were cured of disease. Black Elk said: 'The fear that was on me so long was gone – even the horses seemed healthier and happier after the dance.'

When the world of visions and dreams is neglected, American Indians – like all indigenous peoples – feel uncomfortable, out of harmony with one another and life. By letting each dream or vision image come alive, they allow the emotion of the image to speak, which is exactly what Gestalt therapy is about. When emotional energy is released or unblocked it moves us to live life fully.

Eric Fromm

Psychologist Eric Fromm speaks of dreams as a forgotten language, and says that to people of the past myths and dreams were among the most significant expressions of the mind. His idea of dream symbols is that they are universal, conventional or accidental. Accidental symbols are personal and connected to individual association. Conventional symbols basically mean one thing. Universal symbols – for example, the sun – have universal meanings, such as that of heat and light. Fromm felt that dreams were often dismissed as senseless or not worthy of attention because they disturb us – the person we see in the dream does not fit the person we are sure that we are during the day. Fromm wrote: 'The paradoxical fact is that we are not only less reasonable and less decent in our dreams, but we are also more intelligent, wiser and capable of better judgement when we are asleep than we are when we are awake.'

Arnold Mindell

An approach to dreams very different from that of most analysts is the dreambody work developed by Arnold Mindell, founder of the Research Society for Process Oriented Psychology in the USA. Mindell sees the unconscious – which he calls the 'dreambody' – as a continuously flowing dream, like a river, of which individual dreams are only snapshots. Dreams, physical symptoms, relationships, accidents and altered states of consciousness are all, according to Mindell's theories, manifestations of the dreambody in action. He believes we 'dream up' the world around us to behave like our own dream, and 'call up' certain people to role-play particular qualities in us of which we may not be consciously aware. In this way we experience ourselves in the behaviour of others.

Initially drawn to the field of psychology by his fascination with Jung's teachings, Mindell became bored with talking about the unconscious and archetypes and wanted to see how they operated inside living people – how dreams lived inside the body. Much of Mindell's work involves helping a person go into illness to find the purpose or meaning behind it, rather than to fight it. He does this by amplifying and following pain, feelings, habitual gestures and the patterns of chronic illness until they reveal their hidden dreambody message. He says: 'I prefer to see disease as a dream trying to come into consciousness. When a person goes into the experience, it's almost never illness, but some intense dreambody process trying to happen.' Mindell believes that the dreambody is an active agent constantly expressing itself in our lives, not merely through dreams or illness, but also in every moment of every day, and that most of our problems come from not harmonizing with it.

6

ETHNIC DREAMING TRADITIONS

While psychiatrists and therapists try to get us in the West to look at our dreams and to reconnect with our dream world, the indigenous peoples have never been cut off from it. When an Australian Aboriginal, for example, becomes separated from his dreams, he loses his sense of identity – his identity within the family group, the community and the tribe. Dreams are a fundamental part of their everyday living.

During my travels I have been lucky enough to spend time with Australian Aboriginals, American Indians and African Xhosa, and I have learnt about some of their sacred dreaming traditions.

Aboriginal Dreamtime

Let me tell you about one of my earliest encounters with the Aboriginals. They are so different from us, so old a race, and we can learn so much from their customs.

My dream

The night was so dark that I felt suffocated by its blackness.

Although I was alone, I felt that around me were myriad invisible shapes and shadows who talked, moved and lived as if I did
not exist at all. I wondered where I was, what had happened to
me. Maybe I was dead. I felt as if I had fallen through a hole in
time and become stuck between dimensions. I wanted to move,
but a strange paralysis gripped my limbs. Little flurries in the air
around me made the hairs on the back of my neck stand on end.
My heart pounded with a strange combination of fear and
excitement.

A face emerged out of the blackness and hovered above me.
Brown, ageless, deeply scarred with all of life's joy and pain, it
was the face of the world from the beginning of time. It searched
my soul. My arms and legs began to tremble uncontrollably.
There was nowhere to hide. I was naked, vulnerable and about
to be judged. I felt weak and faint, as if all the strings that held
me together had been cut and I was no more than a heap of
disembodied bones.

The darkness around me lifted a little, and I saw the surface of
the planet so parched and dry that huge cracks had appeared in
it. From the cracks seeped blood, and I heard the earth scream-
ing like a woman in childbirth. A voice said: 'Why do you not
honour what is sacred? Why do you ignore your ancestors, the
sun, sea, earth and sky? Why have you forgotten nature and the
spirit that lives in its every creation?' In that moment I felt old,
young, male, female, black, brown, yellow, red, white – I was
the human race called to account for the sickness of the earth.
But before I could speak, a tidal wave rose up and engulfed me.
The last thing I saw as my consciousness left me was the brown
face of the world searching mine for an answer.

When I opened my eyes again I saw the same face staring at
me from a television screen in front of the chair in which I had
fallen asleep. I gazed back. Behind him on the screen rose the
vast shape of Ayer's Rock – Uluru as it is known to the
Australian Aboriginals – and I felt reconnected to ancient echoes
of myself. Ayer's Rock is a sacred monument, a powerful, living
being and the site of many tribal ceremonies of the Aboriginals,
who consider it to mark the centre of the world.

Was this a coincidence, or was fate playing games with me? I was in Sydney, working; three days earlier, while I strolled the streets of the city, the owner of this old, brown Aboriginal face had appeared beside me. I felt a hand on my arm. 'We've been watching you,' he told me. 'Your work with healing, crystals and dreams is part of our work, our tradition, our Dreamtime. We would like to invite you to join our Aboriginal sisters in Arnhem Land to learn how they prepare for initiation.'

Electric shocks ran through my body. This was not the only seemingly mystical experience I had had recently with Aboriginals. Three weeks before, I had become ill in Queensland. I cancelled my workshops and two doctor friends lent me their holiday cottage on the coast to convalesce. While walking around the fairly isolated area I discovered a piece of land whose limits were defined by cliffs and sea, and whose earth seemed to pulse under my feet. I fell in love with this patch of ground and wanted to own it with a passion unique in my life. After many enquiries I finally found the owner and, without having the means to do so, offered to buy it. It was not for sale. In spite of this I spent every day of my convalescence on it swimming, walking, praying and dreaming: strange dreams in which huge tidal waves rose up out of calm seas to spit the bones of my ancestors at my feet before swallowing me up. I watched the sun rise and set, and felt the spirits of the place heal my body and soul.

Every day I was there alone, until two days before the end of my visit I found a small encampment of Aboriginal women on the edge of the cliff. They came down to the beach; our paths crossed and we smiled. My thoughts were full of going back to work, so I was unaware of a woman who had left the group and come to speak to me. She gestured at the land, sea and sky and asked me if I liked it. My passion poured out as I tried to describe the effect this area had on me. She told me it was land sacred to the Aboriginals, and, although they no longer owned it, they hoped to do so again one day. As she spoke a cockatoo screeched, and the noise jolted me into remembering the tidal wave of my dreams. 'Isn't a tidal wave going to swallow this land?' I asked.

She looked amazed. 'It's quite true,' she answered. 'In our

Dreamtime legends a great tidal wave indeed swallows this land, but when we do not know. It could be in two years or two thousand.'

In the hotel room, my eyes on the television, I wondered if there was some deliberately organized connection between the woman I had met in Queensland and the man who had approached me on the street in Sydney and who had now reappeared on the screen in front of me – or was it a highly significant coincidence? Had my desire for the land, which had turned out to be Aboriginal sacred ground, pulled these people, and this particular television programme, into my life?

I reflected on the power of dreams and imagination, and the ability of indigenous peoples to tune in to these dimensions as if they were as real as those of ordinary life. They, like prehistoric man, value dreams, omens, visions and telepathy and use them as an aid to survival, often effectively. Almost all of them revere the dreaming process, and frequently change their behaviour as a result of dream experience.

Today, instead of relying on his inner senses at least in part, modern man tends to switch on the radio or television and pick up the telephone to obtain information about current events, people and the weather from which to orient his life. These instruments, together with many other machines and gadgets we are so fascinated with, are in reality only outer reflections of the inner abilities we all have. But instead of respecting them, most of us have let them atrophy, and as a result we feel cut off from one another, the earth and nature. It is not difficult to reawaken these abilities, and I am quite sure that if finding a place to sleep at night and a crust of bread to eat depended on our using them, we would be quick to do so. Many of the indigenous peoples I have spoken to believe the white race to be dry and empty, cut off as we are from a sense of the inter-relatedness of all life, and having forgotten the power of dreams and visions. In 1970 Lame Deer, a North American Indian from South Dakota, said: 'God no longer speaks to them [the white men] from a burning bush. If He did they wouldn't believe it, and would call it science fiction.'

'Science fiction' is what I thought myself when I listened to some of the stories of shamanic or medicine men's initiation which I was told during the years following my initial contacts with the Aboriginals. In the end, because the invitation was for six months, while I had a working schedule fully booked for three years ahead, I was unable to go to Arnhem Land. However, even these few meetings brought me close to a number of Aboriginals from whom I learned a great deal.

The television programme in which my new-found friend appeared and gave me such a shock showed the Australian Aboriginals as a semi-nomadic race who wandered across limitless stretches of country hunting and collecting food. They believe in a god usually known as Baime – sometimes Daramulin or Nurundere. He is a very old man who lives in the sky, surrounded by huge quartz crystals and fresh water. Known as the Father of All Things, he is associated with puberty rites and the initiation of medicine men. He often appears in dreams as the master of life and death who can heal the sick.

The role of a medicine man

A friend of mine, who was travelling around Australia and stayed in Darwin for six months, told of a meeting with an old Aboriginal who initially claimed he was a tribal elder, then that he was a medicine man, and later still that because of alcohol he had lost his power. He related that when he was a child he had begun to have strange dreams in which snakes took him on journeys into the underworld. Although the snakes did not harm him he was very afraid of what he saw with them, which included the spirits of the dead who had not lived good lives. Then he dreamed of flying on the back of the Rainbow Serpent up into the sky. For the Aboriginals this belief derives from a story in which the rainbow descended to earth as a serpent whose huge, wide body created paths, streams, rivers and mountains as he slithered across the world when it was new. Offering shelter to two boys hiding from the rain he opened his mouth and accidentally swallowed them, whereupon they changed into rainbow-coloured Lorikeets and flew away. Since then the rainbow has been known as the symbol of spiritual transformation.

On the way into the sky, the old Aboriginal whom my friend got to know was stopped by a crocodile, which spat out the dismembered parts of a child's body and told him he could go no further until he had made the child whole again. The boy tried to blow on the child, but nothing happened. Then he tried to stick the body together by holding the limbs, and finally he called through a hole in the sky to ask Baime to send a spirit to help him. There was a rushing sound and hundreds of small birds and animals came tumbling out of the hole. The crocodile erupted in terrifying cackles of laughter as it opened its mouth to swallow them all, including the dreamer.

Sick with horror and helplessness, he awoke to find himself sweating profusely and with strange marks on his body. His father went to fetch the medicine man, who examined the boy and talked to him about his dreams. He told him he was destined to be a medicine man – or Mulla-Mullung – himself, but he was not yet ready. Before leaving, he made cuts in the boy's wrists and ankles and inserted crystals, which 'gave him a warm feeling and helped him to see into peoples' bodies'.

For many months he was ill and during this time his dreams were full of journeys to Baime's house in the sky, where his ancestors taught him Corroboree songs (a Corroboree is a gathering where songs are sung for the dead) and how to call up the spirits of trees, birds, flowers, animals and the elements. It was on the back of the Rainbow Serpent that he usually made these dream sky journeys – the rainbow being a powerful symbol of initiation and transformation for Aboriginals, who see it as connecting heaven and earth – although occasionally he described being lifted up by threads that hung from the sky.

Not all these dream visits were pleasant. Sometimes Baime appeared as an avenging god threatening to destroy him. At other times he was a kind, benevolent old man who could heal by his touch. As the boy got better, the medicine man took him into the bush and taught him how to expel and reabsorb the crystals he had placed in his body, and how to use his mind and magic words to draw them from the earth. He was shown how to pull out of people objects that seemed to make them sick. After many more dreams, in which spirits and animals appeared to help him, and years of training, he was empowered to become a Mulla-Mullong.

At first he was quite successful and, according to his story, people began to come to him for healing. Usually his dreams told him when they were coming, what was wrong with them and how to heal them. However, he began to drink, after which his healing power waned. Instead of giving him information and guidance, his dreams now began to warn him that he was in danger of losing his power. In one such dream he saw his head chopped off, and when he tried to find it it kept rolling away under a bush. A bird, a laughing kookaburra, said: 'Ha, ha! You've lost yourself!' Although he understood the dream, he could not stop drinking. Finally he dreamed that his medicine bag was taken away, and when he awoke he found that it had indeed disappeared. He never found it again. After that he was unable to heal, and drank even more, because he felt he had thrown away the best part of himself.

During the six months that my friend, Ted, talked to this man he was told many extraordinary tales. Ted was never sure where the dream stopped and reality began, but after a while he did not even care. As the old Aboriginal described his own physical and psychological transformation, as he wove together inner and outer, ordinary and extraordinary worlds, Ted felt himself undergoing transformation too. He had always been a highly practical, down-to-earth man, but gradually he became aware of things that lay hidden under the surface of our three-dimensional world. He began to understand that there were many planes of experience, and that it was arrogant to deny their existence just because he had not participated in them.

The mystery of the Dreamtime

The Mulla-Mullung might have lost his power to heal, but my own life and dreams were enriched by the power of his stories, which stimulated me to explore the dreams of indigenous peoples. Although civilization has dramatically changed the lives of Aboriginal tribes, many of them continue to value their dreams today. Dreams connect them to what they call the Dreaming or the Dreamtime, which describes the creation of the world at the dawn of time, and the mythical beings who breathed life into it. The Dreamtime weaves together past, present and future, without any foreseeable end, and shows the inter-relatedness of all creation. Aboriginals believe that, although the beings who created life on earth have died and moved on, their spirits continue to exist in nature and can be identified in certain rivers, trees, mountains and lakes. These spirits can be contacted in dreams and their energies invoked to improve the Aboriginals' daily lives. For them, man, the spirits of the ancestors and supernatural beings are interdependent and mutually sustaining. Ceremonies using certain instruments, the rainbow and the Rainbow Serpent connect people to this, the Dreamtime.

Aside from ceremonies to honour and invite the spirits forth, they can also appear unbidden, manifesting in both dreams and waking life, especially when a medicine man is being called to follow his vocation. One man had two water-babies, who appeared out of a water-hole and came to help him with his work: they sat on his shoulders and told him what to do, as visible to him as the physical world is to us. Unfortunately, he had an accident and fell head first into the sea. As a result the water-babies, who could not cope with the sudden impact of the salt water, disappeared, and the man lost his power to heal.

The dreams that decide a medicine man's profession usually show him put to death, then taken by the Rainbow Serpent into the sky where he is healed and filled with magical powers. This kind of story, which often features physical dismemberment and psychological disintegration – a crisis of death before a miraculous resurrection – appears in many countries and seems to be an essential ingredient in the training of an indigenous healer. His sickness, madness or breakdown forces him to heal himself before he is allowed to heal others.

Another way of keeping the Dreamtime alive is to go walkabout, a sacred journey following in the paths of the ancestors which can take many months, even years. I have never been on a proper walkabout, but I have spent days in the bush with Aboriginal friends, who showed me how to find Witchetty grubs, berries, fruits, grasses and herbs on which to live. Witchetty grubs are not the most appetizing looking food, but each one contains as much protein as a large steak and tastes a little like chicken. During these trips I joined in ceremonies to induce rain, to avoid disasters such as bush fires, and to give something of ourselves back to nature in gratitude. I met Aboriginal healers and artists, and watched how bark painting is done. I was shown how to use crystals to realign spinal vertabrae, and experienced the effects of a 'magic pointing bone' on my spine when it was sore.

These bush visits loosened me a little from my civilized conditioning and made me more sensitive to nature; my dreams became extraordinarily vivid. Sitting around a fire late into the night, listening to fantastic tales of dreams and visions told in as matter-of-fact a way as we might talk about the events of a day in the office, made me feel part of this forty-thousand-year-old tradition. I learned how isolation, semi-fasting, walking, dancing, chanting and humming can induce dreams and visions, and I found that listening to the recounting of other people's dreams stimulated my own to an incredible pitch.

One night I dreamed that my hands were glowing like embers. The following day two people, in separate incidents, told me that my hands were on fire and that I should use them for healing. A third person then came and asked me to put my hands on him, 'because they are alight and I need their warmth'.

Away from the others, I put my right hand on his chest and my left on his back. I closed my eyes, and after five minutes sensed a terrible turmoil in his chest with something like a snake coming into my right hand. It took all my strength to keep pulling it out, and as I did so it coiled itself further and further up my arm. It was not a physical snake, but the energy of deep repressed rage against his father since childhood. Eventually I felt his chest grow empty and clean, and he began to cry.

I opened my eyes to find us surrounded by a circle of absolutely still and silent birds. They continued to watch us with bright, beady eyes until I threw the snake-like energy off my arm and into the air. The birds lifted as one; they appeared to take it in their beaks – as if I had thrown a live snake – and then carried it away. It was one of the most profound experiences I have ever had.

The power of Aboriginal women

I lived in Australia for twelve years, and during this time it seemed to me that most of the ceremonies to bring rain and to promote fertility of the land and the race, and the rites of passage that lead to initiation and empowerment, were male affairs – perhaps because through menstruation, pregnancy, birth and the menopause women already have their own natural rites of passage, and need no other. In fact, some rituals are so secret that women are forbidden, on pain of death, to witness them. This is not to say that women are powerless: they simply have a more subtle way of achieving their aims. The following story was told me by a group of Aboriginal women.

There was once a tribe whose women worked very hard. They tilled the field, grew the crops and organized everything that went on within the tribe, while the men lay about talking, smoking and drinking. The women owned the power, which was kept, with many sacred objects, in a cave. One day, through dreams, they discovered that the men were plotting to steal their power. Calling together a council of wise women, they decided that, as this information had come to them through dreams, they should ask for a dream to show them what to do. As a result they were told that unless the men were allowed to steal the power they would not value it. Therefore it was better to pretend that they were unaware of the plot until half the power had been stolen, when it would be appropriate for them to step in and claim the other half for themselves. This brought peace to the tribe.

Before the Europeans came to Australia there were some five hundred Aboriginal tribes occupying the continent. Since then civilization has decimated them. In the late 1960s, when I had my first contact with this amazingly rich culture, I saw that to live with the Dreamtime gave an Aboriginal a strong sense of identity, which he loses when he moves out of it. I became fascinated with other indigenous cultures whose dreams were a basis for their psychic and physical growth, and curious about the effect of dreams on world history, religion, literature and art. I saw that dreamers who regarded dreams as important, and even as vital for their survival, not only dream but also dream important dreams which they remember. They also tend to be more balanced psychologically.

The Malaysian Senoi

A good example of a dream-based culture is the Senoi – a primitive tribe living in Malaysia. Much of our information about them is based on the research of Kilton Stewart, an anthropologist and psychoanalyst who lived in Malaysia and studied the Senoi for several years. I have also read Patricia Garfield's book *Creative Dreaming*, in which she describes her own meetings with them. In talking to staff at a local hospital she was told that the Senoi lived in such harmony with one another, as well as with neighbouring tribes, that they had never been known to fight.

The Senoi's reputation for psychological balance stems from their work on dreams, whose meaning will guide them in the decisions they make in tribal life. As soon as they can speak Senoi children are encouraged to share their dreams, first with the family, who will question every aspect of a dream, and later with the tribe. Because so much time is spent in discussing dreams, there is no question of a Senoi not having or remembering them. If a Senoi child dreams of being attacked, his family encourage him to go back into the dream and face the attacker. He can call on dream friends for moral support, but he must resolve the problem alone, even to the point of killing his opponent if necessary. (The Senoi believe that, by 'fighting to the death' in a dream, a positive energy is released from the part of the consciousness that formed the dream image.) The idea is to confront and conquer danger, and to shrink problems to a manageable size by facing up to them. The children learn that the only thing to fear is fear itself, and that running away only makes it worse.

Young Senoi are encouraged to explore and experience every dream situation to its conclusion, including flying, falling, drowning, kissing, petting and sexual intercourse – the last three because the Senoi believe that the dreamer cannot have too much love in a dream. Senoi children are prompted to ask for a gift at the end of a dream if it was happy, and to *demand* one if it was threatening. In other words, by learning to bring their dreams to a positive conclusion Senoi children grow up understanding that every event in life, too, can have a successful outcome.

Dreams come alive for the Senoi because they bring into the day what they saw at night. For example, they wear the colours that appeared in the dream, sing the songs, speak to friends, and carry out community projects as suggested by the dream. Unfortunately, with civilization encroaching on their culture the Senoi people are no longer what they were when Kilton Stewart lived among them in the 1930s and 1940s. But this in no way invalidates their dreamwork, which can be as effective for us and our children as it was for the Senoi themselves.

Children love working with dreams and, through using the Senoi techniques of confronting and conquering danger, experiencing every situation to its completion, develop the ability to handle their problems. Many of the children I have worked with had a fear of falling, and always awoke in great distress when this type of dream occurred. By guiding them through the dream, encouraging them to keep falling until they hit rock bottom in order to see what was there, I helped them to overcome the fear.

Some children described landing on coloured cushions, in trees or in strange landscapes. Others landed on flying carpets, feathers, sand, crystals or the backs of animals, or were caught by magical friends. They received gifts ranging from unicorns to rockets, from puppies and kittens to chemistry sets and exotic jewels. Afterwards the children drew what they had seen in their imagination; this reinforces the experience and helps children to remember the dream for future use. I have done this with large groups of children who, as well as working with their own nightmares, did so with one another's. It was amazing to see, not only their transformation, but also the excitement and creativity stimulated by dream-sharing.

African Tribal Dreams

Some of the most successful workshops I have given along these lines were in Africa, which since my childhood has been the subject of many of my dreams. When my feet first touched African soil and I caught a glimpse of thatched huts, black faces and the vast open stretches of land and sky, I felt as if I had come home. When I entered a hut for the first time I 'knew', as if my life had been spent in one, what it was like to cook in a pot over a fire in the centre of a room, and to feel my bare feet on the mud-packed floor. Whether this was *déjà vu*, reincarnation or a dream memory coming alive I do not know, but I had to pinch myself hard to make sure that I was physically present.

A young black girl in a house where I stayed told me that in her tribe dream events were handled as if they had happened. If a man seduced another man's wife in a dream, or committed what was considered to be an offence within the tribe, he was punished as if he had done it literally. As a child this girl, uMeri, dreamed she was bitten by a scorpion, and was treated exactly as if she had been bitten. She said that tribal members sometimes drank herbal infusions to stimulate dreams, although most of this ritual was the province of witch-doctors, medicine men and Sangomas – a mixture of sorceress, medicine woman and herbalist.

uMeri believed that when she was asleep her soul left her body, and she was sometimes afraid that it might not find its way back. In fact many years later I read that, because of the prevalence of this belief in some parts of India, it was made a capital offence to paint someone's face when they were asleep in case the dreamer's soul could not recognize the right body in which to return.

Becoming a medicine man

There are hundreds of African tribes, each with its own particular centuries-old customs and rites. Just as dreams call the Mulla-Mullung of Australia to his profession, so they play a vital role in calling a Zulu, for instance, to become an Inyanga (a shaman or medicine man). Dreams are believed to be visits from friends and ancestors coming to warn or guide, and they begin to shake the future healer out of his previously accepted role in life. When the spirits begin to whisper in his ear, telling him what to do and how to behave, he usually becomes seriously ill or appears to go crazy, sometimes both, and can take many years to recover.

During this time, again like the Australian Aboriginals, many of his dreams will include death, dismemberment or disembowelment, flying, song-singing, the appearance of animals, birds and mystical beings, as well as spirits and ancestors, out-of-body experiences (see p. 138) and visits to the underworld. In the process of initiation into his profession the future Inyanga or Sangoma undergoes a complete breakdown of his physical, mental, spiritual and emotional senses. During his training he lives between various worlds, often becoming a semi-outcast to his family and tribe who must endure his erratic behaviour until his exploration of these worlds, and himself, is complete.

Although their tribal upbringing has taught them to revere and obey their dreams and visions, some medicine men (and women) who are called in this way by the spirits have a strong resistance to the summons. This results in an inner conflict which often brings about or prolongs illness, sometimes increasing the severity of the symptoms, and can last a lifetime if the person refuses to respond to the call.

In one place that I visited, a local witch-doctor very unexpectedly (especially as we could only communicate through smiles and gestures) gave me an anklet made up of stones, feathers, string, dice, bones and other bits and pieces that together created a magic totem of power and protection. He said: 'I recognize you', which was translated to me. This stimulated friends to refer to me jokingly as 'The White Muti' (Muti means medicine). As a result a Zulu cook, far away from his family and homeland and working for friends, approached them to see if he could send a woman from his tribe to see me, 'because a great sickness is upon her'. Somewhat apprehensively I agreed to see the lady, who I then discovered had been trained as a Sangoma.

At fifteen she had been orphaned; shortly afterwards the local Inyanga told her that he wanted to teach her to carry on his work after he had gone. Awed by his attention, she went with him. She told me that he was very good to her and that, as well as the discipline of a hard and sometimes frightening training, she also learned from him how to laugh. The people of the tribe accepted that she would eventually carry on his work, and when she was nearly fifty her teacher and mentor died. However, she had spent so many years being his assistant that she forgot she was expected to stand in his shoes. The first time she had to perform in this role she panicked, feeling that she was nothing without her teacher beside her. But that night he came to her in her dreams and told her not to worry. She need do nothing except let him occupy her body, so that he could continue his mission. Despite her training, she suddenly became both resistant and frightened.

In the following months she did her work, but also tried to keep her Inyanga teacher from entering her body or her dreams. She began to feel increasingly inadequate, and finally decided that she could not carry the mantle of knowledge he had passed on to her, let alone share it with others. She tried to go back to normal tribal life, but it was very difficult. The people were afraid of her, just as she was afraid of herself. After a time she began to lose her sight. Urged on by the combination of spirits and revengeful images of the Inyanga in her dreams, she resumed her Sangoma ritual and practice. Again she became frightened, feeling that both her teacher and the people she was supposed to help demanded more from her than she was able to give. So she relinquished her role completely.

When she came to see me she was almost totally blind. During our conversations together – she spoke perfectly adequate English – which included invoking the spirits, it was made very clear to both of us that her blindness was the result of her 'refusal to see' and 'carry on with' what she had been trained to do. As she denied the power of her inner sight, so her outer sight diminished. She battled with the spirits, but finally settled for blindness and ill health rather than follow what they wanted her to do.

I heard a number of stories about African healers who converted to Christianity and as a result tried to free themselves from their spirit helpers. In nearly every case they lost their power to heal and brought misery and misfortune into their lives. Their belief that the spirits were angry and upset, and therefore caused their problems, was far more deeply ingrained than their new-found belief in the power of Jesus Christ.

The dream culture of the Xhosa

The first workshop I gave in South Africa was on a farm whose land was originally the site of a practising Xhosa witch-doctor's sacrifices and rain-making ceremonies. An extraordinarily powerful energy seemed to pulse out of the ground, stimulating the senses so that our dreams and meditations became highly charged and significant. I was told by someone who knew a little about the traditions of the Xhosa – one of the oldest and best-known black tribes in South Africa, who have used dreams for thousands of years to direct and guide their lives – that there were two types of dream, social and personal. A social or 'big' dream was the more important, because it affected the wellbeing of the entire tribe; for example, it suggested when to move to another area, or to make a sacrifice to invoke success in war or hunting.

I wondered if dreams were still as important to the Xhosa today, and tried to find books on the subject. Then I met a psychologist named Robert Schweizer, who had spent many years living with and studying the Xhosa. He told me that despite his South African, American and English psychoanalytical training he had learnt more about psychology from the Xhosa than from any other source.

For the Xhosa, dreams are a means of communicating with the shades or spirits, who give practical help, healing and advice. One Igqira – a cross between a witch-doctor and a psychic healer, in other words a shaman – stated: 'You never awake a child, or any person, for while someone is asleep he is communicating with the shades.' He added: 'If you dream that you are bitten by dogs, you do not tell anybody. You just prepare beer. The dog is your protector. Anything which is protecting you which is biting you shows that the shades are quarrelling with you. The beer is begging peace with them. You have to think what wrong you have done, and the beer will allow them to tell you.'

Robert said that the major difference between Jungian dream interpretation and the Xhosa tradition is that the Xhosa actualize their dreams and live them out to the point that animals are slaughtered, journeys made and beer put out to appease the shades. Often a man's work will change as a result of dreams. In fact, if instructions given in sleep are not obeyed, 'bad things will happen'. As one Xhosa healer told Robert, 'You are fast asleep, and you get told what to do in your sleep. If you do not accept, you may lose your home or die. There are other things – you may become restless, a drifter.' He also said it was important to dream of an animal, which then becomes 'your' animal or dream totem. 'My animal is a lion. The lion stands for my grandfather. If I infringe one of our laws, this lion comes into my dreams in an aggressive manner.'

The Xhosa believe that people are born healthy and that illness is caused by separation from the shades, by failing to make the proper sacrifices, or because a person has been bewitched. Aside from the Igqira medicine man/witch-doctor/healer there is also the Ixhwele or herbalist, whose medicine cures all sorts of ailments including love problems, and also protects against evil. The basic difference between the Igqira and the Ixhwele is that the former is a diviner, seer and psychic, a mediator between the ancestral spirits and the living, whereas the Ixhwele is trained in a practical way in the use of herbs. Another type of shaman is the Igowina or sorcerer, a man or woman who creates potions to cause harm, even death, to people, property and animals. He is greatly feared because 'he can send things into you'.

Tom, who worked on a property near where I stayed, believed he was afflicted in this way, and despite many visits to his Igqira and Ixwhele deteriorated so fast that his boss brought his own white doctor to see him. The doctor found nothing physically wrong with Tom, but could see that he was mad with worry. Phambana, the Xhosa word for madness, is caused by failing to follow the customs (in other words, making sacrifices), which leaves a person open to attack from an Igowina. Tom then dreamed that the Umamlambo, Mother of the River, could heal him – the People of the River play an important role in Xhosa mythology – and the following day went down to the river and threw himself in. He disappeared completely – his body was never found – and his family believed that he was healed and living with Umamlambo, who is a river-snake spirit. They expected him to return one day as a great Igqira.

Tom did not throw himself into the river to commit suicide as we might think. His state of mind, his phambana, convinced him it was the only thing to do. He lost his identity by not following the Xhosa tradition and rituals in which he had been brought up, just as the Australian Aboriginal loses his when he steps out of the Dreamtime.

By contrast a friend of Tom's, Sidzumo, who began to behave as if he too were suffering from phambana, recovered completely by doing exactly what the Igqira told him to do. His case was different because he had not been bewitched, but the initial symptoms of his illness were very similar. However, the Igqira told him he was suffering not from phambana but from Thwasa sickness – separation from the shades, which is nearly always experienced when in his dreams a man is called by his ancestors to become an Igqira. It signifies conflict and crisis, a disintegration of the personality, hence its surface similarity to phambana.

Initially, Sidzumo became quite ill as his inner and outer

selves battled with what he had been called on to do. His limbs ached and shook with an almost continual tremor. He slept little, and when he did his dreams were full of terror and dread. He then dreamed that his mother came and told him to slaughter an ox. When that was done, the people should build a house for him.

When he awoke, these actions were carried out, and the house built exactly as his mother had specified in the dream. He began to feel better, and, realizing that the only truly lasting cure was to accept his call, he became an Umkhwetha, or initiate. His calling affected his whole community, and his training took place against the background of its support. In fact, without it he would never have found the courage to embark on his new vocation. His initiation into his new role could not take place until he had openly accepted his illness in a public ceremony. This meant that he 'owned' or 'identified with' what he had previously struggled to deny and feared. In other words, he faced his own shadow, or dark side, and by so doing began to accept it.

During his subsequent training, ceremonial rites, which included much singing, clapping and dancing, helped him to channel the energy of chaos into harmony and creativity. He learned to respect himself and his ancestors, reforging his links with them through dreams, sacrifice and ritual. Sidzumo saw in his dreams a variety of animals, as well as people he had never met before, but who claimed to be members of his family. When he described them to his father and grandfather, they were able to identify and name each person.

The word Thwasa literally means 'emergence' or 'coming out' and indicates a kind of rebirth that is repeated many times throughout an Umkwetha's training before he emerges as a qualified Igqira. Sidzumo spent three years learning and another two as an assistant before he felt ready to call himself an Igqira. He said: 'Thwasa is something in the blood, a gift from the ancestors. You can buy knowledge of herbs, but you can't buy Thwasa. If you don't follow it, it will follow you.'

Robert Schweizer generously allowed me to read his thesis on the Xhosa, now in the University of Cape Town library; it gave me a greater understanding of the two cases I have described. The way he talks about Thwasa treatment, which uses dreams extensively, can help us all:

> *The individual takes over and possesses the daemonic, by which he had previously been possessed. He confronts, comes to terms with, and integrates the daemonic into the self system. This process strengthens the self because it integrates what has been left out. It overcomes a paralysing 'split' of the self, by integrating the potentialities and other aspects of one's being with behaviour. It brings together the conscious and unconscious aspects of the personality. When this aspect (the shadow) is denied, it is the source of hostility and aggression, but when it is integrated via consciousness into the conscious personality it becomes an enlivening source of energy and vitality.*

This could be a description of modern psychological treatment, yet it has been practised by the Xhosa for thousands of years.

Listening to your izibilini

On a far more basic level, I discovered many Africans – victims of a migrant labour policy which forced them to leave their homelands in search of work – who use their dreams to keep in touch with the health and wellbeing of their families far away. If a dream suggests that things are not going well at home they will try to get back there themselves, or send a message via someone else.

Nomadinga had been gardening for friends of mine for some twenty years when he decided to take another wife, considerably younger than his first. That caused immediate trouble, from which he tried to dissociate himself by returning to work as quickly as possible after his occasional visits home. However, his dreams were the source of constant crisis, and after days of holding his stomach and complaining that his izibilini, his intestines, hurt, he would set off home in a melancholy fashion to see what was wrong. He finally pacified both wives and his izibilini by arranging separate houses for each woman.

Sebukaki, a Kenyan houseboy, had recurring dreams in which he was told, he believed by God, to kill the cook. He would get up, seize a large, shiny knife and hurl himself at the cook, who always managed to take to his heels in the nick of time. Fortunately he had a faster turn of speed than Sebukaki. The friend who told me this story says he has vivid childhood memories of Sebukaki and the cook tearing round and round the house like blurs of light until they were both exhausted. Peace reigned until the next dream, and happily for the cook, Sebukaki eventually returned to his village.

The tribal African walks conscious of the earth under his bare feet. He listens to and acts on what his dreams and intestines tell him – in fact Africans believe they are ruled by their intestines (or 'gut' feelings), while white men are ruled by their brains. The African grows up with a sense of interconnectedness between himself, his ancestors, his fellows and all of creation around him – as do the American Indians.

American Indians

Like most indigenous peoples, American Indians believe that through dreams man is called upon to follow a certain path in life. My first contact with these people came about in a curious way. Feeling cramped by the lack of space in London, I went to Cornwall for a few days to walk and realign myself with the land. There I discovered a number of stone circles, and walked round them musing on their mysteries and the sacrifices that might have been made near them.

One circle consisting of twenty-one stones – a large stone in the middle surrounded by twenty smaller ones – had a particular fascination for me, and I returned to them again and again. The middle stone, which was almost as tall as I was, had the air of a neglected woman who needed attention. I made a small bouquet of wild flowers and laid it at the stone's base. Suddenly I remembered a miniature bottle of Cornish mead in my pocket and, opening it, sprinkled some on the stone. To my amazement, it seemed to come to life and glow. From where I stood I threw a little mead on each of the other stones. They too lit up.

I was now standing in the centre of what looked like a wheel of light whose illuminated spokes extended from the stone hub to every stone on the glowing circumference. I felt as if I was in the middle of an American Indian medicine wheel – a framework reflection of heaven and earth, and, like the mandala, a powerful focus of meditation between spirit and matter. Before leaving, I walked around the perimeter of the circle three times, and was even more astonished to find a small clump of American Indian headdress feathers. On my way back to the car I found more and, somewhat bemused, drove off.

An hour later I found an olde worlde English pub in an equally olde worlde English village, to which I felt very drawn to stay the night. I went into the dining room and my mouth fell open when I saw in front of me a group of American Indians wearing their ritual feathers. Almost immediately we began to talk. They told me about ancient Hopi prophecies coming out of dreams and visions that predicted many events that have since taken place, such as the arrival of Europeans on the American continent, the two world wars, the dropping of the atomic bombs and the Americans' landing on the moon. These prophecies also spoke of a time of cleansing, 'when the earth would shake with great earthquakes, volcanoes would erupt, there would be great storms, and fire and ice would strike'. Many American Indians I have spoken to since then believe that we are now in the time of cleansing, and that survival is possible if we return to the ways of the sacred teachings.

These Hopis had come to England to perform ceremonies of prayer and healing for the Earth Mother on which we live, and they had held one ceremony at exactly the stone circle where I had been. They hoped to bring harmony to the land wherever they went by talking to the Great Spirit, Father Sky and Mother Earth, by invoking the spirits of the grandfathers and grandmothers, and the forces of air, water, earth and fire. They spoke of forces on earth reaching out to speak to people and said that it was imperative that we should pray for dreams, vision and inspiration to make these messages clear to us so that we can act on them. I learned, in fact, that the idea for their own travels had come from a number of what are called Vision Quests, under-taken independently by each member of the group.

The Vision Quest

Because a Vision Quest is embarked on primarily to discover a person's life task and the animal which will be his guiding spirit, the first Quest usually takes place around puberty. Just as the Senoi learn to work with their dreams as soon as they can talk, so too are native American Indian children, boys especially, prepared for their Vision Quest. It is a sacred rite of passage that initiates a child into adulthood and from which he finds his place in the community.

The ceremony itself lasts from three to four days, during which the boy undergoing the Quest must remain alone, unclothed except for a blanket, and without food or water. Before this there is a great deal of preparation in which dreams, meditation, fasting, solitude and finally time in a sweat lodge all play a significant part. Purification of body, mind and spirit is essential, in order to allow the true dream or vision to reveal itself. Although each American Indian tribe has rites unique to its own tradition the Vision Quest seems common to all; it comes from the belief that solitude and suffering open the mind, and that true wisdom can only be found away from other people.

Just as I had felt part of the Aboriginals' ancient history in Australia, now, as I talked in Cornwall to an American Indian, I felt as if I were within an American Indian skin. As Little Dog shared his memories of waiting day and night for a vision which he feared might never come, my imagination put me in there with him. I suffered his fear and apprehension, felt the beat of his shivering heart as the cold and the dark crept in on him, and jumped as he jumped when the night owls screeched. I winced at the thought of his little sister cutting squares of skin from her arms, which she had then wrapped up carefully and given him in a gourd, to remind him that he could draw on her courage if his failed. His thirst and loneliness became my experience, so that when Little Dog described the sweat lodge that preceded his Vision Quest I was undergoing that with him too.

His father and two uncles made the sweat lodge out of bent willow saplings, blankets and tarpaulins. (I later saw one: it looked a little like an Eskimo's igloo, very low on the ground, so that you had to crawl to get into it.) Little Dog's father made a fire pit in the middle of the sweat lodge, prepared the sacred pipe and told Little Dog to spread sage on the floor; in the Indian tradition, sage purifies and makes sacred. The stones to heat the lodge, which had been used many times before, were already in a brightly burning fire outside.

Little Dog, his father and uncles took off their clothes and crawled inside. They lit a bunch of sage and waved it about, each person praying that Little Dog would be worthy of having a good dream and a good vision. Gradually the red-hot stones from outside were passed in and placed in the fire pit. Little Dog began to feel hotter and hotter. His mind felt loose, as if strings attaching him to everyday life were melting away, and he thought he was going to faint.

Suddenly his uncle threw ice-cold water on the burning stones, and the lodge filled with scalding steam. Little Dog thought his lungs would burst. More stones, more steam – he would die, he was in fact dead. Images rose up before him – people he had known, or had never seen before, animals, birds, plants. He felt himself falling, flying, shrinking, expanding, dying and being reborn.

Suddenly his father touched his elbow and said, 'It's time to go.' He handed Little Dog the sacred pipe and told him he must never lie about his vision or anything else, because it would bring trouble on his people. Little Dog inhaled his first tobacco, savouring the taste and praying for a vision to make his father proud of him. He knew that the tribe and the medicine man, who would later help him to interpret his dreams, were all waiting to see how his vision would define his place in the tribe. He felt strange and light-headed, and did not know if he had been in the sweat lodge for hours, days or weeks. He emerged, staggered to his feet and followed his father up the hill to the vision pit – a pit dug into the earth and covered with branches, grass or leaves.

It was very dark and very cold. Little Dog's father wrapped him in a blanket, made specially for Little Dog's first Vision Quest by his grandmother, gave him the gourd containing his sister's flesh and the sacred pipe they had just smoked, and left him. Little Dog said that the first night in the vision pit was the worst. He felt completely alone, and although he knew that the spirit spoke through trees, plants, stones, rocks, animals and elements, he was as apprehensive about what might manifest as about what might not.

Tears poured down his cheeks, his arms and legs became numb and he was very thirsty. After a while his whole body felt numb and his mind seemed to float above it. He prayed, clutched his gourd and pipe for courage, and drifted in and out of dreams where shadowy shapes, both animal and human, tried to talk to him. He lost all sense of time, and eventually his dreams and visions became as clear as if a physical presence had taken him by the arm and was telling him exactly what to do. Little Dog said that what occurred during those four days and nights had changed him from a boy to a man. When his father came to fetch him, even his voice seemed deeper.

I spent the next two days in Cornwall with the Hopis, sharing in ceremonies to consecrate and bring balance to the land, listening avidly to their stories and determined to undertake my own Vision Quest as soon as possible. I again realized that, when dreams play a vital part in the lives of a people such as the Aboriginals, Senoi, Xhosa and native American Indians, they all do in fact dream. It would not occur to them to say that they never dreamed, or did not remember their dreams, or to toss them aside as irrelevant – as many of us in the West do.

An Indian named Lame Deer, who is now dead, once said: 'Crying for a vision, that's the beginning of all religion. The thirst for a dream from above – without this, you are nothing, I believe.'

7

DREAM INCUBATION

The Rites of Ancient Egypt

Lame Deer speaks of white men creating a desert within themselves because they no longer cry for a dream. This was certainly not true of the ancient Egyptian and Greek priests, priestesses, prophets, wise men and magicians who were able to use dreams to move into other worlds, just as the medicine men and women of primitive tribes can still do even today. Through dreams they transformed themselves, healed the sick, divined the future and communicated with the spirits of the dead.

Many of my childhood dreams, fantasies and hypnagogic images depicted palm trees, pyramids, mummies in sarcophagi, hieroglyphic writings on papyrus scrolls, feluccas skimming the Nile and fellahin solemnly ploughing the earth while ibises and cranes stood expectantly by for upturned worms. I felt as if I knew what it would have been like to grow up in Luxor at the foot of the Valley of the Kings, with the Temple of Karnak a mere stone's throw away. Through an Egyptian school friend, whose father and grandmother had a deep knowledge of the ancient Egyptian world and its beliefs, I was able to share some of its mysteries.

The priests and priestesses of Memphis and other well-known temples and oracles, such as Isis, Khimunu, and Thebes, all practised dream incubation: they were highly trained in the use of ritual, ceremony and spiritual discipline as a means of invoking the gods to heal the sick through dreams and visions. Although dream incubation today is a way of asking questions and receiving answers, in the past it was associated with sick people who were brought into the temples; here they purified themselves, fasted, prayed and often took drugs to induce healing dreams. To ensure a god-inspired instead of a demon-provoked experience during sleep there were dozens of prayers, formulae and incantations to be recited, and amulets to be worn to ward off evil and give protection. Bes, the Egyptian god of sleep, was supposed to send good dreams and to keep demons away. An old papyrus says that to ensure its effectiveness an appeal to Bes should be written in ink 'made from the blood of a white dove, mulberry juice, cinnabar, rainwater and myrrh'.

The Greeks and Their Oracles

The Egyptians assimilated a great deal of their attitude to dreams from other societies and earlier civilizations. In turn the Greeks borrowed heavily from the Egyptians, also believing that dreams were sent by the gods, and that the soul travelled in sleep and had adventures which prepared it for life after death.

In Greek mythology the god of sleep, Hypnos, and the god of death, Thanatos, are twins, representing two sides of the same condition. Although the Greeks believed that dreams were god-inspired they were also afraid of demons, and used herbs, amulets, magic spells, prayers and incantations to protect them during sleep. Dream interpretation was popular, and the ancient Greeks consulted favourite priests and magicians to decide whether a dream was good or bad. A 'good' dream was acted upon – the 'bad' needed a cleansing, protective ritual.

Homer, the Greek writer and philosopher, described the Gates of Ivory and Horn through which dreams came. According to Homer, dreams that were 'true' and 'good' passed through the Gate of Horn, while dreams that 'deceived' or 'deluded' passed through the Ivory Gate. Sleep itself was revered

– it was a mystery that led to communion with the gods – and the Greeks had many ways of inducing it. Incense, drugs, herbs, meditation, fasting and hypnotic exercises were all used in the temples to loosen the consciousness from its objectivity. It was believed that when someone was completely relaxed – in a trance, asleep or even in a state of ecstasy – the spirit was more likely to have a vision or mystical experience.

The oracles, central to the Greek mysteries, were famed for their pronouncements which, despite their ambiguity, were believed to be divinely inspired. Today if we want to book a holiday, buy a house or take a new job we have myriad agencies to help us. The Greeks had the oracles, whom they consulted on subjects ranging from religion, art, philosophy, science, war and peace to more personal issues of love and hate, birth and death. There were oracles in temples, caves and grottoes all over Greece, and most of them used hallucinatory drugs and stupefiants in their rituals.

The oracle at Delphi is probably the best known. Here the priestess inhaled fumes coming from a vent in the ground, and when she was in a semi-tranced, intoxicated state she would answer the questions put to her. The oracle priestesses were young virgins trained to develop psychic abilities and kept apart from the others within the temple to ensure the purity of their contact with the gods. They became symbols of truth, wisdom and mystery.

Today the use of drugs and intoxicants is considered to be a social evil, an escape from reality that, if abused, can deaden our feelings and cut us off from life. In the past, priests, priestesses, teachers, shamans and holy men both took and administered a variety of drugs, including alcohol, during prescribed religious ceremonies. Instead of cutting them off from life, the dreams, visions and fantasies that resulted were a source of growth, wisdom, strength and renewal. Today we use the word 'fantasy' to dismiss something as irrelevant or unreal. It comes from the Greek word *phantasía*, which means 'to imagine', 'to make visible' or 'to reveal'. *Phantasía* enables us to 'make visible' other worlds by creating images that give them form. Robert Johnson, the Jungian analyst who wrote *He* and *She*, concerning

the use of myth in the evolution of male and female consciousness, says:

> *The human mind is invested with a special power to con-
> vert the invisible realm into visible forms so that it can be
> seen in the mind and contemplated. We call this invisible
> realm the unconscious. For Plato it was the world of ideal
> forms; the ancients thought of it as the sphere of the gods,
> the region of pure spirit. But all sensed one thing: only our
> power to make images enables us to see it.*

For the Greeks, *phantasía* or imagination was the means by
which the gods 'spoke to man' – it was through *phantasía* that
dreams occurred, and so the Greeks would do anything to
stimulate it. Ceremonies to arouse the imagination and induce a
sense of euphoria included art, music, movement, dance, acting
and mime, which were as important as the use of herbs, incense
and intoxicating drugs.

The gods and goddesses of the Greek mysteries were as much
a part of Greek family life as were brothers and sisters, cousins
and aunts. Regular sacrifices and daily offerings were made in
temples dedicated to Zeus, Apollo, Dionysius and Pallas Athene.
Plays were performed, re-enacting many Greek myths, and the
deaths of Adonis, Dionysius and Orpheus were mourned by
'official' days of weeping.

The Greeks had a deep understanding of the psychology of
their invisible worlds, which we would call the unconscious. The
temple rites and ceremonies, the pageantry and theatre that lay
behind everyday births, deaths, marriages and socializing, were
carefully designed routes into these worlds. With such a background, it is small wonder that the Greeks were so successful in
using dreams to cure the sick, or that dreams became such a
highly developed art within the healing temples.

Most of the healing temples were dedicated to Asklepios, the
Greek god of healing, and probably the most famous of them is
at Epidaurus. Asklepios was a man who really existed, around
1100 BC. His symbol was a snake, and even today the caduceus
– a snake coiled round a staff – is an international sign for

medicine. In Asklepios' time dreams were the foundation of physical, psychic and spiritual growth and health. Like the oracles, dreams could answer questions on every imaginable subject. To invoke or incubate a dream within a temple or grotto was a sacred rite requiring intense preliminary work. In fact, this preparation was a prime cause of the dynamic results of Greek dream incubation therapy.

How the ancient Greeks incubated dreams

Imagine for a moment that you and I were living in ancient Greece and we became ill. We would first consult the oracles, soothsayers and herbalists, and make pilgrimages to holy sites and sacrifices to the gods, before invoking the help of Asklepios. The decision to do this was similar to the one we might make today to go into analysis or a course of psychotherapy. It was a serious commitment that triggered anxiety. Admission to the healing temples was forbidden unless one was invited to enter by the god of healing himself in a dream.

To encourage Asklepios to appear in our dreams we would have to cleanse and purify ourselves with herbal purges, a strict diet or fasting, prayer, meditation and hours of solitude. We would have needed to surrender ourselves to the moon's power (the power of the unconscious) by sleeping under her rays and bathing in springs and streams which we had first cleared of rocks and debris to ensure that their waters flowed freely. We would have had to abstain from sexual intercourse, listen to the priests in the temples, and beseech the goddess Astarte, who held the power of life, death and health, or Sophia, the goddess of wisdom, to help our minds wander into the world of the gods, whose powers could bring bright visions.

These procedures are very similar to those followed by American Indians preparing for a Vision Quest. They not only heighten sensitivity, but stimulate such a strong expectation that something will happen that it usually does. Although the 'dreams of invitation' sometimes showed Asklepios as he was depicted in many of the statues and engravings within the temples, he could also appear in symbolic form as a snake. No matter how he appeared, these dreams were interpreted with priests and, if considered genuine, allowed the applicant into the outer temple, where he incubated his first healing dream.

Again, long hours of preparation were involved, including physical exercise, the inhalation of herbs, the witnessing of profound musical and dramatic performances, and the making of sacrificial offerings according to the celebrant's means. The subtle effect on his feelings and senses harmonized his body and soul. As the lamps were dimmed he lay down to sleep encircled by the statues and pictures of Asklepios. He heard the scuffle of the sacred temple snakes slithering over the floor and the rustle and breathing of the people near him.

Memories of inscriptions put up in gratitude by those whom Asklepios had cured filled his mind. One at Epidaurus described how a man from Thebes was covered with lice. He dreamed that the god undressed him, took a broom and brushed the lice away. When he awoke he found the lice gone. Another account told of a girl, paralysed and unable to leave her bed, who sent a friend to the temple to incubate a dream on her behalf. That night Asklepios appeared to the paralysed girl, saying: 'Why aren't you in the temple?'

She replied: 'I cannot move.'

'Well,' said the god, 'then I'll have to heal you here!'

When morning came, she awoke and found that she could walk. Was the same miraculous healing possible for our supplicant?

Lying on his mat as darkness fell, he must have felt apprehensive and expectant, disoriented by all he had seen and done. No doubt he prayed fervently to the god Hypnos to grant him sleep, and to incubate a good dream in which Asklepios cured him. To go to sleep in this way was not only of itself a magical experience, but also produced results. Within the temple, dreamers were encouraged to wake up after a vivid dream, memorize it, and then go back to sleep in the hope that a further dream would help clarify the first.

The hours just before dawn were considered the most propitious for what was a form of re-entry into the dream. Most ancient people thought of this time as a marriage between the sun and the moon, a doorway merging the two worlds, conscious and unconscious, visible and invisible. It was during these hours that Hermes conducted the souls of the dead to the underworld, and it was the most fertile time for dreams and visions. (Even today, more babies are born and more deaths occur at this time than at any other.)

Perhaps our dreamer, having told his dream to the attendant priest, drifted back into an early dawn sleep and now, praise be to the gods, Asklepios appeared. This was no longer like a dream. The supplicant, hearing Asklepios' voice, scrambled to his knees in ecstasy. He saw the god clearly in front of him and suddenly felt a sharp pain in the diseased part of his body. He tried to touch Asklepios' sandalled foot, but fell back in a semi-faint. He awakened to find himself healed, and described what happened to the priests and fellow dreamers before giving thanks to the god. If he had not been healed, he would wait to be invited into the inner temple.

Dream incubation rites had the same effect as hypnosis or hypnotic suggestion might have on us today. Over the years hundreds of people, including our imaginary friend, had dreams and visions in which Asklepios appeared and cured them. Some were healed overnight during sleep. Others were told exactly what to do and, provided they followed the instructions precisely, were also cured. The temples were in a sense forerunners of modern hospitals and clinics. A priest was a true physician – a combination of healer, teacher and priest – who understood that health depended on an integration of body, mind and spirit. He was well trained in dream interpretation and used dreams to diagnose mental and physical disturbance, often before it had manifested in the body. Many years later, when psychoanalysis was born, doctors began to develop new ways of treating the sick and realized, like the priests and healers before them, that dreams contained important clues to the real cause of illness, and that if the cause was treated correctly the symptoms would disappear.

Incubating Dreams Today

Although within the healing temples dream incubation rites followed an elaborate ritual, dream incubation became so popular that it was considered quite normal to go off to a lonely cave or hilltop and invoke dreams to solve everyday problems. The basic principles of preparing oneself, asking for help, healing or insight, and going to a sacred or peaceful place to sleep are as valid for us today as they were for the ancient Greeks: dream incubation still works. We can create a sacred space around our own beds or even in our imagination if there is nowhere else to go. Candles, crystals, flowers, herbs or incense, prayers and music all help to build an atmosphere in which we can relax and dream. To invoke a dream is to invoke our unconscious to speak. If we invite friends to the house we usually take a little extra trouble to make them feel at home; we need to do exactly the same for our own inner selves.

Without knowing what I was doing, I began to use dream incubation when I was a rebellious pupil at a convent school. I spent much of my time sent out of the classroom for inattention or mischievous behaviour. I missed so many lessons that examination time was always a last-minute flurry of panic and study. I would put notes under my pillow, believing that in some magical way my dreaming self would memorize them for me. It always worked, and I still do it today if there is information I need to remember. This led to my writing down and literally sleeping on questions to which I wanted direct answers.

A friend, Agi, once wanted me to accompany her to India to visit her teacher's ashram. Because there were only two tickets left she told me I must decide within twenty-four hours. Half of me wanted to go, while the other half was unsure. So I wrote on a piece of paper: 'Is it in my best interests to go to India or not?' and slept on it. In the resulting dream I slid down a mountain of red-tiled roofs to land in a heap at the teacher's feet. He leaned forward and gave me a handful of jewels. I looked up to thank him and saw to my astonishment that, while everything else in the dream was brilliantly, almost gaudily, coloured he was like a black and white photograph. I always dream in colour, and I had never before seen black and white in a dream. While I was still in shock at his monochromatic appearance against the background of an arch of flowers bursting alive with colour, he leaned forward, took the jewels and turned away to give them to Agi. It was very clear that what the teacher had to give was not for me at this time. I did not make the trip.

In addition to asking my dreams for an answer, if I am not sure what to do I often use the Increase/Decrease prayer. I say silently in my head, or aloud, or even sometimes write down: 'If it be Thy will and in my best interests – or for my highest good – to have this/ go there/ do such and such, please increase the desire in me. If it be against Thy will and my highest good, decrease the desire in me.' It always works, and I usually get some sign of confirmation too.

For example, some years ago I accepted an invitation to do a three-month workshop tour of Australia. Two weeks later friends invited me to join them on an all-expenses-paid holiday in Sri Lanka, where I was born. I yearned to say yes, but of course I had to honour the prior commitment. In addition the Sri Lanka trip was a holiday for pleasure and enjoyment – surely selfish in comparison to the duty and responsibility of my Australian visit. So I said no to the holiday, but because the Australian visit was planned twelve months ahead I decided to use the Increase/Decrease prayer too.

During the following days I became more and more excited about thoughts of going to Sri Lanka. Every travel agent I passed appeared to have windows decorated with smiling Singalese faces, waving palms and turquoise lagoons. Even my local supermarket participated in a Sri Lankan/Ceylon tea promotion! Wondering why my desire to go was so much increased when my Sri Lankan trip seemed an impossible dream, I began to think that for the first time the prayer had not worked. Suddenly through my letter-box popped a letter from Australia saying: 'Dear Soozi, it would really suit us better if we could postpone your visit for four to six weeks.' I went to Sri Lanka and had a wonderful time, revisiting my old home and many familiar places. I then continued to Australia for my work.

To ask a dream for insight, information or healing, to use dreams to solve problems, is as valid for us today as it was for the ancient Greeks and Egyptians. In Chapter 3 I explained how you can ask for a dream, or incubate a dream, to help you solve any problems you may be facing in your life. They help you get in touch with your inner child. A friend of mine, Betty, used her dreams to help her lose weight. As a result of dream incubation and lucid dreaming (becoming aware that you are dreaming while in the dream), she was able to find the *cause* of her problem and deal with it. To her family's amazement, within six months she was back to the slim shape she had had at twenty.

Another friend, Caroline, the third wife of a man considerably older than herself, suffered dreadfully from feelings of jealousy, anger and insecurity. After trying many other therapies, she began in desperation to work with her dreams. A year later, I barely recognized her. Using her dreams to learn about herself, to explore many hidden fears and forgotten childhood feelings that lay beneath her jealousy, had helped Caroline to be herself and not what she had thought other people wanted her to be. At forty-eight, she was finally in charge of her life. She told me: 'I've learnt from my dreams that no one can teach me as well as I can teach myself. I'm more confident with other people, more open about myself. I have found an inner security I never had before.'

A source of knowledge

An extraordinary case of modern-day dream incubation is that of Ahmed Youssef Moustafa, an Egyptian, who had an unshakeable belief in the validity of his dreams. They were meaningful and highly practical, and provided the magical inspiration for his life and work.

Ahmed was a child of the streets, a waif who stole food in order to survive. He was completely at home in the pyramids at Giza and not afraid of upsetting an *akh* or spirit. While sleeping in the pyramids, he had recurring dreams of ancient Egypt. In these dreams he learned how the pigments were mixed for painting pictures, statues and mummies. He saw how the hieroglyphic characters were inscribed on the walls, and understood their meaning. At nineteen, Ahmed, illiterate but streetwise, discovered that the Cairo Museum was looking for someone to restore artefacts from the pyramids and rebuild the skeleton of a boat buried by the Cheops pyramid. He applied for the job and tried to explain that his knowledge came through his dreams in the pyramids. But he was laughed at and told to go away. The Cairo Museum advertised all over the world for an 'expert restorer', but no one knew how to rebuild the boat.

Ahmed returned to the Cairo Museum time and time again, saying that he knew how the boat had been made, insisting that the slabs of the hull had been sewn together. Every time the officials laughed and sent him away. Eventually, the Egyptian authorities challenged him to rebuild the boat, and to their amazement he did so. This boat, supposed to be the one that carried the Pharaoh to the underworld, is now completely restored and can be seen displayed alongside the pyramid of Cheops. It is big, extraordinarily graceful, and of great beauty, and it was recreated to this perfection as a result of one man's dream.

Ahmed was subsequently invited to work for the Cairo Museum, and has probably spent fifty years of his life there. Another of his remarkable achievements has been to restore many of the prehistoric paintings on the pyramid walls, which had disintegrated into dust when exposed to light and air. Ahmed's childhood dreams had shown him exactly what to do. And if he was ever in any doubt, he would go and sleep in a pyramid in order to receive a clear and practical dream answer.

8

DIFFERENT KINDS
OF DREAMS

Whether incubated, lucid, prophetic, warning, recurring, telepathic, a nightmare or 'ordinary', dreams can put us in touch with a source of wisdom, inspiration and direction that can stimulate us to decisive choice and action. They are gifts from the inner to the outer self, and contain messages uniquely designed for the dreamer. If we listen to them they reward us with the gift of a second life. In the words of the American writer Thoreau: 'Go confidently in the direction of your dreams. Live the life you've imagined.'

Past Lives

Despite scepticism in the West, many people from other cultures believe in the concept of reincarnation. Professor Ian Stevenson, who has devoted a lifetime to investigating the subject, says that scientific proof of reincarnation is no more than ten years away. The idea of rebirth and karma is basic to most Eastern religions, and the present Dalai Lama is supposedly the reincarnation of his predecessors. In Richard Bach's book *Jonathan Livingston Seagull* an older, wiser gull, Sullivan, says to Jonathan:

Do you have any idea how many lives we must have gone through before we even got the first idea that there is more to life than eating, or fighting, or power in the flock? A thousand lives, Jon, ten thousand. And then another hundred lives until we began to learn that there is such a thing as perfection, and another hundred again to get the idea that our purpose for living is to find that perfection and show it forth. The same rule holds for us now, of course; we choose our next world through what we learn in this one.

Edgar Cayce, who gave thousands of past life readings, did not initially believe in reincarnation. Finally the overwhelming evidence in its favour, coming through his own readings, caused him to change his mind. Cayce subsequently believed that each soul has subconscious access to characteristics and skills accumulated in past lives, while also being subject to the influence of lives ruled by negative emotions like fear and hate.

The value of past life therapy

Past life therapy is now an accepted way of curing physical and psychological problems that refuse to respond to more conventional treatment. The major difference with past life therapy is that it gets to the root cause, whereas other methods treat the symptoms.

In my own work clients often remember other lives, which always leads to a dramatic improvement in both their health and attitude to life. Also, by getting an overview of what has contributed to whom they are today they acquire a better understanding of their present life choices, patterns, relationships, work and interests. Remembering another life can sometimes open up forgotten pain and trauma, but at the same time the release of blocked energy cures problems. The process of individuation is to be in touch with all our parts or aspects of ourselves, but also every experience we have ever had. By bringing these to consciousness we expand our power to live.

Searching for clues and getting in touch

Dreams, *déjà vu*, and instant rapport with or dislike for a complete stranger can all provide clues to previous lives. To look at an atlas and decide which place on it attracts you the most, or to scan the history books to see what historical period, clothing or activity seems most familiar or interests you the most, are also points from which we can begin to explore the past.

For example, I have always felt drawn to and comfortable in France. Books on the French Revolution used to churn my emotions, even at school. One day I meditated and then mentally asked for a dream to show me if I had lived in France at the time. I saw myself as a somewhat languid lady, living in a chateau amongst an enormous collection of musical boxes. From here I was unceremoniously dragged off in a tumbril to have my head chopped off. In my dream I felt such terror as the guillotine crashed down that I woke up. Some years later a psychic, who knew nothing of this story, described the same life to me – including the musical boxes – and added that I had been guillotined twice: the first time the blade had come down on my jaw, and not on my neck. The blow to my jaw must have left a strong impression, because all my current life I have been plagued with jaw problems.

Another way of getting in touch with past lives is to stare at yourself in a mirror by the light of a candle or a shaded bedside lamp. You must initially concentrate on staring into your own eyes for at least five or ten minutes – longer if your face has not begun to change by then. You will gradually see a variety of other faces begin to emerge from your own and then dissolve into the glass again. These can be male, female, young, old, happy, sad, aggressive or wise – the variety is limitless.

When you feel there is a particular personality you want to explore more deeply, or with whom you sense more of an emotional connection, close your eyes and dialogue with it in your imagination. Ask any questions that help to give a composite picture of that life, and listen inside for the answers that will come floating up into your mind.

If you have never done anything like this before, you may

need to practise sensing the images, words and feelings that your imagination lays before you. Do not *judge* what comes, and do not think that you are making it up. What comes into our imagination originated in the unconscious. The imagination enables us to see what would otherwise be invisible by giving it an image; like fantasy, it makes visible or reveals what already exists.

I find it helpful to ask: 'Who were you before? Where did I know you before?' as if I were talking to someone else. In fact, I have often used similar techniques in workshops by getting two people to sit and face each other, knee to knee, while they stare into each other's eyes. It can be extremely difficult, and after five minutes people are often either in tears or hysterical with laughter. If they persevere, and silently ask the same type of questions, the partners' faces change, and the information about past lives that comes tumbling out is usually quite extraordinary. Another way of starting off if your mind goes blank is to close your eyes and simply think of yourself as a friend with whom you have agreed to do such an exercise. Say: 'Once upon a time, X...' and make up a story as you go along which leads you to the life you are trying to research.

Encountering past lives through dreams

Gandhi said: 'It's nature's kindness that we don't remember past births', but in today's world knowing and accepting crucial events of times gone by can transform our present lives. Of course there are myriad ways in which to find out about previous incarnations, including asking a psychic or doing past life regression. The above techniques are simple and effective, but still subject to personal perception in a way that dreams are not. Erlo van Waveren, a therapist and student of Jung's in the 1930s, said that the only way to check the proof of reincarnation is through dreams: 'They are the only proof we have – the dream is the taproot.' Van Waveren wrote a book called *Pilgrimage to Rebirth*, in which he describes some of the lives revealed to him through dreams going back to 700 BC. Dreams telescope past, present and future experience into the immediate now, and give us personal psychic readings of whatever we both do and do not want to know. In my experience, to ask a dream for information about other lives has always brought a response – not only for me, but for others too.

For forty years Pauline endured phantom heart attacks which caused almost as much pain as real attacks. A past life memory coming up in a dream suggested that, as a black magician, she had indulged in human sacrifice in which human hearts were removed from living people. (Strangely enough, Pauline is now married to a heart transplant surgeon.) Although initially distraught by her dream, since having it she has never had another attack.

A fourteen-year-old boy was cured of bed-wetting when he remembered a previous life cut short at eighteen that set up a refusal to grow up in this one. Another child recalled a life in which he ran away, leaving friends to be tortured and put to death. He swore that he would never run away again, and in this life developed leg cancer so that to run was a physical impossibility. Encouraged to imagine reliving his old life, and to forgive the person he was then, enabled him to stop unconsciously punishing himself – as he was doing through the cancer – and within a year he was cured. This does not mean to imply that past life recall is a magic cure for everything, but it does mean that it is another way of finding the possible root cause of a problem, and can give very positive results.

Past life dreams are not always so clearly spelt out nor so dramatic. Some of them simply give subtle hints which, if we think about them, can open up our understanding of the people around us. I have friends whose past-life dreams have shown them why one child is loving and the other antagonistic, why a new-born baby suffers from asthma or a husband or wife leaves home. The confirmation of 'truth' from such a dream is the shock of realization and pain that comes with it, which can include physical symptoms such as shaking, twitching, tears and breathlessness. If the past life recalled was peaceful rather than dramatic, the recognition of truth can come simply as a very strong inner certitude. The truth can also be judged by the way one's life or attitude to it changes afterwards. So many of us repeat the same patterns and problems, and to see these exposed is a dramatically effective way of correcting them. It is similar to the shock of seeing and hearing ourselves on video for the first time. We suddenly become aware of unconscious gestures and body language which helps us change them.

Through dreams and regression, six friends and I discovered we had all been nuns in a convent run by a very strict Reverend Mother who, in this life, is a man married to one of the group. We jokingly call him 'Reverend Mother' because he is still, due to his work, running around organizing the nuns' welfare. Clearly, he just cannot get out of the habit! What is extraordinary about this story is that each of the seven of us independently had this image of him as a Reverend Mother, and of ourselves as the nuns he dominated. At least this little tale illustrates that past-life experiences can have their light side too!

The dream life of Omm Sety

A fascinating example of past-life dreams is the extraordinary story of Omm Sety, an Englishwoman who died only a few years ago. At the age of three, Omm Sety, or Dorothy Eady as she was then, fell downstairs and was pronounced dead. She revived, however, and began to have recurring dreams about Egypt and her relationship with the Pharaoh Sety. These dreams implied that three thousand years earlier Dorothy had been a young girl named Bentreshyt (Harp of Joy) living in the temple of Sety at Abydos. When she was 14 she became an initiate into the Osirion Mysteries and took vows to be a priestess of Isis. Bentreshyt was now temple property, a virgin priestess whom no one was allowed to touch. By accident she met Sety in the temple gardens and, after a number of meetings, they made love. Sety then left Abydos, but promised to return as soon as possible. Before he came back, Bentreshyt, now pregnant, was questioned by the high priest who said that her crime against Isis was punishable by death. Not wanting to compromise the Pharaoh, Bentreshyt committed suicide. When Sety returned he was heartbroken to learn of her death, and swore never to forget her.

Three thousand years later he appeared to Dorothy Eady in her visions and dreams, reaffirming his love and commitment.

Between the ages of 14 and 29, when she left England to live in Egypt, Dorothy's dreams introduced her to reincarnation, astral travel, and life in Amenti – the land of the dead. They reminded her of ancient Egyptian traditions and gave her countless opportunities to talk with Sety. The Pharaoh originally appeared in a mummified state but, after her move to Cairo, gradually revealed himself as he was when Dorothy was Bentreshyt. According to Omm Sety's secret diaries, Sety could manifest himself physically, even to the point of making love to her. Both her mother and her father-in-law caught glimpses of him, and her cats spat and arched their backs when he came into her room.

It was not until Dorothy Eady moved to Abydos in 1956 that she became known as Omm Sety, which means Mother of Sety in Arabic. At last she felt she was truly at home, and, in addition to all her other activities, she unofficially resumed the duties of an Isis priestess, whose vows, according to her dreams, she had made so many centuries before.

Friends who spent time with her said she was warm, practical and down to earth. She was an expert draughtswoman, writer, scholar and healer, with a great sense of humour and a liking for beer. She spoke so fondly of Rameses the Second, Sety's son, that they thought she was talking about a hyper-active child who would appear at any moment.

Omm Sety was consumed by her dreams, and inspired by her unshakeable belief in what they revealed. But she lived them out in a way that enriched her life, rather than cut her off from it.

Big and Little Dreams

Dreams can be described as the theatre of the mind, creating nightly entertainment that absorbs 50,000 hours of an average life. During this time we are presented with an astonishing variety of types of dreams and scenarios. Dreams introduce us to the huge cast of characters we have living inside us and constantly respond and comment on what we are doing with our lives. Dreams never waste our time, and even a small, seemingly insignificant dream – a little dream – tries to tell us something we need to know.

For me a little dream is a personality dream that offers a running commentary on personal issues, whereas a big dream is God-inspired and soul-sized; it expands way beyond personality and usually involves a major change in our way of looking at life.

Little and big dreams are somewhat like minor and major initiations. A minor initiation in life occurs when something happens that is so painful or shocking – we are fired from work, a parent dies or a lover leaves – that we feel nothing will ever be the same again. A minor initiation is often mistaken for a major one, but in fact we stay on in the same house, wear the same clothes, mix with the same friends and continue to live much as before. A true major initiation, such as a change of career or a catastrophic illness, results in such a total change that we are no longer the same person. Our work, home, needs, habits, clothes, likes and dislikes change so much that we barely recognize the person we were before. Because a major initiation comes after many minors we often do not recognize them until months later, when we look back and compare the difference between now and then.

Prophetic and Precognitive Dreams

These can only be judged as such if the events they prophesy subsequently take place. History is full of such dreams. Dreams foretold the future success of rulers such as Genghis Khan, Napoleon, Oliver Cromwell and Hitler. Constantine, before the battle that made him the Emperor of Rome, dreamed of the Cross, a symbol of Christ, and a voice said: 'In this voice, conquer!' He used the cross as an emblem, won the battle and converted to Christianity.

When I was growing up I began to have precognitive dreams in which I saw and experienced events that subsequently took place. Some of them were small things, such as an unexpected visit from a neighbour, or seeing myself at a birthday party amongst lots of children in fancy dress, which occurred in fact exactly as I had seen in my dreams three or four weeks earlier.

Other dreams had much greater impact. In Sri Lanka I dreamed that a snake that lay on the floor of his car bit the local doctor. Even as I write I can still clearly remember the patterns on the snake's body as it slithered away in my dream. Some days later a snake indeed bit the doctor as he got into his car, and he died within twenty-four hours. I dreamed of other people dying, and they often did. I became afraid of going to sleep, in case I was making things happen.

For most of us the dream message is not so clear – so how do we judge between true prophecy and dream fantasy? In my own experience of working with my dreams and those of others, there seems to be a sense of recognition (similar to past life dreaming), a gut feeling that impels one to follow through on what the dream says. For example, we do not catch the plane or train that subsequently crashes. Many of my precognitive dreams concerned my future work and came years before they made sense to me.

Dream researchers say that prophetic or precognitive dreams are quite common, and it is a fact that the more attention we pay to dreams the more psychic we become. In the dream state our ego boundaries dissolve, and it is possible to tune into ideas and events 'waiting to happen' (if I had understood this as a child, I would have been less worried that because of my dreams I was *making* bad things happen). Many writers, musicians and artists pick up their ideas in this way and sometimes produce the same theme, totally unaware of someone else's similar work in another part of the world. When an idea's 'time has come' to manifest in the physical world, there is no restriction on who may pick it up. Before the Second World War many people, including Jung, had precognitive dreams about it. However, even if I dream about war and it comes true, I must still ask myself what this has to do with me and my life. The bombed buildings I see crashing down around me in my dream may be a message to me to let go of some of the old structure of my existence.

Prodomic Dreams

Many such dreams warn us about possible consequences to our health if we continue to eat the wrong food or drink too much alcohol, and can sometimes show us the onset of disease before it starts. Health warning dreams are known as prodomic dreams.

Before developing a chronic lung infection years ago I dreamed that an axe was thrown at my chest, and blood filled my lungs. During their work with heart patients in America, dream researchers discovered that prior to a heart attack male patients frequently dreamed of violence, wars and destruction, while female patients had fearful dreams of separation from what they loved.

A car is often used in a dream as a symbol for the physical body. If the brakes fail, if the engine refuses to start or runs too fast, if the steering locks, or if you have to push the car up a hill (I often have such a dream if I am really tired and run down), if a policeman stops you or gives you a parking ticket, or if the car runs out of petrol, these are all hints to look at what you are doing to your body. I sometimes invoke a dream to assess my physical state. This is not a substitute for seeing a doctor, but it can give me little clues about changing my diet or taking more rest.

Healing Dreams

These can come spontaneously, or may need to be invoked in a way similar to the incubation rites of ancient Greece. This can be done for ourselves and for others, but we must always remember to ask only for what is the highest good of the person concerned. This may not in fact mean physical recovery; it may mean release from the physical body, or an increase in symptoms in order to learn something. Perfect soul health is the ability of the body to experience the symptoms it most needs, to respond to those symptoms and then to move on to a different experience. In other words, it is always a teaching-learning experience. We often learn more through the limitations of illness than we do through health; illness teaches others as well as oneself, and we must never interfere with another person's karma. There are inner plane healing temples to which we can offer our services when we go to bed. We may have no memory of this work when we wake up, but the offer is never refused. We can also visualize a healing temple or room in which we mentally place ourselves and others before we go to sleep.

One night Sue, who had been seriously ill for months, did this, and dreamed that she was taken away by six men in white coats who put her in a garment like a straitjacket. She overheard people around her say: 'Look at Sue. How terrible!' In that instant she knew that she was going to be healed. When she woke up the following day she felt different, and from then on began to get better. Another way to invoke a healing dream is to imagine sleeping in the robe of Christ, which ensures peace and protection during sleep. Whether you remember the details of a healing dream or not, always say thank you in the morning.

Telepathic Dreams

These provide us with information about events happening at a distance, and about which we have no conscious knowledge. For instance, Tessa dreamed that her sister gave birth to twins and one died. Five months later, returning to her family home from many months abroad, she found that her sister had recently given birth to twins and that one had died. Pam dreamed she met her uncle wandering in a wood, where they discussed their lives, hopes, fears and ambitions. Two days later she met her uncle in the street; he said, 'I saw you in my dreams' and proceeded to tell her word for word what they had discussed in Pam's dream.

Dreams of Compensation

These bring emotional balance by letting us live out unlived parts of ourselves – good and bad. Someone with an inferiority complex may dream of meeting the Queen or performing heroic life-saving roles, whereas someone with heavy responsibilities may dream of being a gypsy or a playboy. Through dream incubation we can invite these sub-personalities to reveal themselves to us, and by getting to know them and integrating them into our lives we can use their energy. This type of dream can also introduce us to our inner child (see Chapter X), animus, anima and shadow, and show us how we mutually feel about one another.

Shadow figures in a dream often appear as a threat, a monster or a grotesque figure. The more we repress and hide what we do not like about ourselves, the more monstrous and grotesque our shadow becomes. If we face our shadow, it changes and turns out not to be so bad. If we run away, it will grow. The animus and anima also reflect our attitude to our male and female energy.

For twenty years Anita, now forty and painfully shy, dreamed that she kept a man bandaged from head to foot and tied to a bed inside a locked room. When she eventually began to take a few tentative steps into life, he broke free of his bandages and turned into a two-year-old child who kept taking his pants off and revealing his genitals. When an interfering dream figure told Anita it was disgusting to allow the child to expose himself like this, Anita laughed. She woke up realizing that she was finally exposing her own male energy without embarrassment. Over the years, as her confidence grew, so too did the boy grow up.

Nightmares

What the Chinese call dreams of 'terror and dread' release repressed emotional energy that can jerk us awake, hearts thumping and gasping for breath. In nightmares we are usually running – or unable to run – being chased, pushed, imprisoned, suffocated, or in some way threatened by such monstrous and overwhelming calamity that we wake up to get away.

The best method of dealing with a nightmare is to get back into it as quickly as possible and face it. Imagine being back in the dream again. Confront and befriend the energy; don't be afraid to talk to it. Question it, calling on dream friends if necessary: 'Who are you? What are you? What feeling or part of me do you represent? How can I help you? How can I heal you? How can you help me?' A nightmare demands our attention and tells about our fears. By going into it rather than running away we transform its threats and rob our fears of their power over us. Similar to the Senoi methods of confronting and conquering danger, described in Chapter 6, this type of technique is excellent for children and adults alike.

Some nightmares can have their message interpreted without going back into them. For instance, Annette had recurring dreams of great terror in which she saw herself going to bed in a house whose doors and windows she was supposed to have locked, but had forgotten to do so until she was in bed. Her fear prevented her from getting up and she lay terrified while strange creatures and whistling winds floated and blew through the house below. I asked her if there was an area in her life where she was vulnerable to attack, where she had left herself open. As soon as she recognized and dealt with this, the dreams stopped.

Tim had nightmares in which he experienced his body entangled by octopus-like tentacles that sucked the life blood from his limbs. He was excessively generous, and the nightmares were trying to point out that he was allowing his energy to be drained by the people around him who fed on that generosity, his money – his life blood. Unconsciously Tim realized he was being taken for a sucker, and was upset about it. It took the nightmare to bring it into his consciousness.

Recurring Dreams

Another type of dream that demands attention is the one that repeats. Recurring dreams are often a cry for help from the inner to the outer self. They also indicate a refusal to listen or to change, and need to be treated in much the same way as a nightmare.

I once shared an apartment with Connie, who had recurring dreams in which she walked into an isolated cottage and found a little girl sitting on the floor quite alone, very serious and still. Surprised at the child's presence, because the cottage seemed deserted and dusty, Connie went towards her. Always, before reaching the little girl, Connie heard the most terrible sobbing fill the room – and yet the child herself was not crying.

For years Connie awoke deeply disturbed by these dreams, but never did anything about them. When eventually I offered to guide her back into the dream, Connie discovered a door she had never noticed. On opening it, she found a small boy sobbing his heart out. He was dirty and emaciated and would not let Connie touch him.

Connie suddenly realized that this scruffy, abandoned little boy was herself. As a child she had wanted to wear shorts and climb trees, but her mother had insisted that she wore frilly, feminine, slightly old-fashioned clothes which she was never allowed to get dirty. So she became the quiet, serious little girl she first found in the cottage, while the boy she always wanted to be was locked away and left behind. By going back to the time when her mother had cut her off from an essential part of herself, Connie freed an energy of creativity and adventure which significantly enriched her life.

In the process of dealing with this dream, Connie became enormously angry – the angry little boy ignored and never listened to. Once recognized and released, the anger turned into dynamic creative energy. Usually these lost forgotten inner children guard lost forgotten feelings which must be allowed expression before true healing can take place. As Connie discovered, it is never too late to parent the inner child, and as a result her recurring dream stopped. Journal writing, visualization, inner dialogue and Gestalt are all effective means of doing this. Recurring dreams are like constantly ringing telephones. If we answer their call they can wake us from sleep to life.

Lucid and Pre-lucid Dreams

Lucid dreaming involves becoming fully aware of dreaming during the dream, and is often a prelude to astral travel. For most people this is quite difficult, although it can be learnt. To have a vague sense of dreaming while in the dream – which is quite common – is called pre-lucid dreaming. In a lucid dream we can take charge and change whatever is happening at will, whereas in a pre-lucid dream we do not really know what we are doing.

When we have lucid dreams, in which we realize that we are dreaming and take action which changes what is happening within the dream, we are receiving very important messages. The dream is saying to us 'You can change anything in your life. You can change anything you don't like. You can take charge.'

An American friend had a lucid dream in which he saw his mother carry his eighteen-month-old son up stairs which had no bannister or support rail. He watched his mother trip and begin to fall downstairs with the baby in her arms. Immediately he changed the dream by imagining her safely on the landing at the top of the stairs, across which he also imagined a child-proof gate. He recognized these stairs as being at the back of his own house; they were normally not used.

Awake, he looked at them and, because of his dream, decided to fit both a bannister and a handrail so that, if anyone *did* trip, they could hold on with both hands. A week later his mother, while carrying his baby son up these stairs, had a heart attack. As she fell, she grabbed the rail on either side and managed to save both the baby and herself from falling to the bottom.

Not all lucid dreams are predictive, but they can certainly empower us to take action and assume control over our lives. Carlos Castenada was taught to induce lucid dreaming by staring at his hands for ten minutes before going to sleep. As soon as he began to dream, the image of his hands was supposed to swim up into focus, and to remind him that he was dreaming, so that he could take charge of the dream. Many people find this procedure, a form of auto-suggestion, successful.

Anything that we personally choose to use as a reminding trigger will do. Dream researchers have discovered that flying is often a part of lucid dreaming, so one way to induce a lucid dream is to concentrate on flying just before going to sleep. The sensation of flying, drifting and floating is also associated with astral travel, so lucid dream preparation often leads there.

Alan Worsley, a psychologist and guinea pig for a lucid dream research team in London, discovered as a boy that by calling his mother's name while dreaming he could wake himself into lucidity. He produces on demand lucid dreams in which he carries out prearranged activities which are monitored on tape. Alan says: 'If I can levitate or push my hand into the table I know I am dreaming. Also the colours and imagery are extra sharp and bright. I have a lot of fun flying over landscapes, water, doing acrobats and flying backwards – in a lucid dream you can transfer yourself wherever you want to go.'

Another lucid dreamer conjures up in his dreams friends with whom he can stroll on the beach or fly about. He did not like one such companion's attitude, so he said: 'You're only a figment of my imagination, and if you don't pull yourself together I'll wake myself up and you'll disappear.'

His companion retorted: 'Then you'll find that you're only a figment of my imagination too!'

Sexual Dreams

Lucid dreams stimulate sensitivity and sexuality, sometimes to the point of orgasm. Sexual dreams, whether lucid or ordinary, stimulate creativity and symbolize union with different parts of ourselves, as well as with our own divinity. If we dream of making love with someone of our own sex, we are reinforcing and merging with our own male and female energy, as well as with the qualities of the man or woman represented in the dream. Instead of feeling guilty or embarrassed by such dreams we should joyfully accept them, knowing that by so doing we will become much more spontaneous in our sexuality and in our whole way of living.

The ancient Greeks and Egyptians used sexuality within their temples to arouse the fertilizing powers of the gods. It was considered the highest form of human expression, a sacrament uniting the human with the divine. As a result, both were nourished. We too can arouse the fertilizing powers of the gods – which means to stimulate our highest potential – by incubating sexual dreams in which we, like the Senoi, 'advance towards pleasure' or orgasm. We can also dedicate any sexual experience, both in and out of dreams, towards the expression of these powers, which will not only increase sexual pleasure but also inspire creativity.

9

DREAMS OF DEATH AND ASTRAL TRAVEL

What you can do, or dream you can, begin it,
Boldness has genius' power and magic in it.
GOETHE

The Inner Stranger

In Greek myth, the archetypal story of Aphrodite and Psyche reflects the struggles and challenges which we all have to face in life. Aphrodite, the goddess of love, was angry and jealous when her son Eros, the god of love, fell in love with Psyche, a mere human. The story is about the warring of these two women, and can be interpreted as the warring between two aspects of ourselves, one of which is strong and confident, and the other fearful and inadequate.

Aphrodite told Psyche that unless she fulfilled certain tasks she, Psyche, would die. The first task was to sort the seeds of the world overnight. The second was to gather fleece from the Golden Fleece. The third was to get water from the River Styx, and the fourth and final task was to go to the underworld and get a jar of beauty cream from Persephone, Queen of the Underworld.

Aphrodite set Psyche these tasks one by one. Each time the task seemed impossible to fulfil, and Psyche wept and wailed and prepared to die. When faced with sorting the seeds of the world overnight, she decided that she might as well drown herself in a river. But on the river bank she met Pan – from which comes the word panic – who told her not to worry; he would send ants to do the job for her. When Psyche told Aphrodite the task was done, Aphrodite, instead of congratulating her, wanted her dead and sent her off on her next task. Again Psyche, ready to kill herself, was helped, this time by an owl. The owl told her that she could avoid danger by waiting until dusk when she could take all the fleece she needed from the hedgerows where the animals had rubbed their backs.

Aphrodite then sent Psyche for water from the Styx's raging torrent. An eagle helped her this time. He took the crystal goblet in his beak, saying that he could fly over the river and fill it for her. Now Psyche had only to go into the underworld. She had two coins to pay the ferryman for her journey there and back, and was advised to give no help to anyone on the way. She was also to take her own food, because if she ate food from the underworld she would never return. She followed this advice, but on her return, at the last minute, was tempted to open Persephone's jar of beauty cream, and she fell unconscious. Eros, god of love, awakened her, and with Aphrodite's agreement had her made a goddess.

The story, of which I have picked out only a small part, is one of growth and transformation. It is about the evolution of Psyche's consciousness, as a model for humanity. Her four tasks are initiations, through which we must all pass if we wish to achieve maturity.

The first initiation, to sort the seeds of the world, means to learn discrimination, to assess our priorities and *choose* what we accept and reject. The second, to gather the golden fleece, means taking enough male energy to do what we need to do, but no more. If we take too much we become aggressive and tread on other people's toes. The third initiation, to fetch water from the raging torrents of the Styx, symbolizes moving out into the market-place of life; if we do not have a clear idea or ideal (the crystal goblet) of what we want, life will wash us away. We can fill as many goblets as we want, but without a goal what we do is worthless. The final task of going to the underworld means to be willing to explore the very depths of ourselves, to face and come to terms with what we are in our innermost beings, and what we fear the most. By so doing we can discover our own beauty. Crucial to this final task, however, is the advice given to Psyche, not to give help to anyone on her way. In other words, she was told to hold on to her power and not give it away. If she gave it away she would never achieve what she was meant to in life.

This may sound cruel. It does not mean that we must *never* help another human being. But it *does* mean that, as illustrated by Psyche's first task, we must discriminate between when to say yes and give help, and when to say no. Frequently the 'no' catalyses a crisis which can ultimately be more healing than the 'yes' which may well collude with the problem.

Our equivalent of Psyche's tasks are not always easy to undertake. Psyche's feelings of impossibility and despair are something I have experienced many times myself, and each time dreams have given me the push to get on. Psyche was helped by an owl and an eagle. The owl symbolizes intuitive wisdom and the eagle the power to ascend, to see from a different and higher perspective. By using these qualities Psyche was able to act with greater initiative than before, and consequently accomplished incredibly difficult tasks. The powers of the owl and the eagle – and much more – are available to each one of us every time we go to sleep and dream. Dream power can help us to face life's challenges with boldness and daring so that we, like Psyche, can break out of the invisible barrier which has locked us in what William James called 'a very restricted circle of our potential being'.

Jung once described this inner power and wisdom as 'another we don't know' living within us. 'He speaks to us in our dreams and tells us how differently he sees us from how we see ourselves. When we find ourselves in an insolubly difficult situation, this stranger within us can sometimes show us a light which is more suited than anything else to change our attitude fundamentally.'

Sometimes this 'stranger' can appear as an actual person – mine appears to have a variety of disguises, ranging from an angel to St George and a man wearing a safari suit, pith helmet and dark glasses, who leaps about the jungle with a butterfly net in one hand. Often the dream itself is the guide, without the involvement of a particular personality. For example, a man came to me for therapy after he had nearly killed his ex-wife's lover, Russell. Even though Ted and his wife had been separated for two years, he was still very jealous. He spent weeks plotting how to murder Russell, and the day finally arrived when he was ready to execute his plan. But these plans had to be postponed when, on the way to Russell's house, Ted's car broke down.

That night Ted dreamed that a policeman came and showed him the complete scenario of the plot, in which Ted hid in Russell's house and then beat him to death with a crowbar. Stooping to make sure that Russell was dead, Ted found himself staring at his own lifeless face, which was so badly beaten up that it was only just recognizable.

When he woke up Ted had no recollection of the dream, but drove to Russell's house, climbed in through an open window and waited for Russell's return. Everything went according to plan. But as Ted was about to strike Russell his dream came flooding back to him, and the memory stopped him in his tracks. The two men subsequently sat down and talked about their mutually antagonistic feelings.

Ted's dream wisdom did not issue specific instructions, but helped Ted to change his attitude fundamentally. When Ted told me the story he was particularly amazed by the policeman's non-judging acceptance of what he was about to do. We must always remember that this inner teacher-guide is there to help and guide us, not to judge and punish us. He stands by as witness to our full potential and, no matter what we may or may not do, directs us towards it. A policeman in a dream is often an angel in disguise and, as with Ted, can give us a little nudge to reconsider what we are about to do.

Many of the world's greatest thinkers acknowledge the presence of inner guardian-observers. Socrates, who was told by an oracle that he was the world's most knowledgeable man, had an inner guide described as a 'private patron' who knew him 'most intimately'. Apuleius, when writing about Socrates, said that to the person who seeks to know and honour him, this guiding figure will communicate 'now through a dream, now through a sign', or that this guiding figure can even step in to 'lift up the soul in defeat, steady an inconstancy, lighten our darkness, and direct what is favourable towards us'. Jung himself talked to Philemon, a guru-type figure who appeared in both dreams and waking fantasies. When describing him, Jung said that psychologically Philemon represented superior insight: 'To me he seemed quite real, as if he were a living personality – I went walking up and down the garden with him.'

Preparation for Death

If dreams and dream guidance can change our entire attitude to life so fundamentally, they can prepare us gently for death as well. Phillipa's 21-year-old son 'accientally' died from falling off a balcony in Chile. Neither family nor police were ever sure if his death was the result of a drug-intoxicated leap or a deliberate murder. Six months later Phillipa, almost suicidal after her son's death, dreamed that she flew in a plane to a beautiful but foreign country where she saw her son practising baseball with a friend. As she walked towards them her son rushed to greet her, saying: 'Look how well and happy I am!' Before she could open her mouth to agree, he introduced her to his friend, and told her that they were building a house for her to live in when she herself 'arrived'. She woke up with a feeling of great happiness that her son was in such good health, combined with a sense of expectation about the beautiful white house which she would eventually live in near him. Twelve months after this dream Phillipa was diagnosed as having brain cancer. She also discovered that her son's baseball-playing friend was in fact dead when she had her dream, a fact she could not then have known. Phillipa tried valiantly to fight her brain cancer, but ultimately she went happily to her son. Dreams had guided her mercifully to that deep peace.

Dreams about death can take many forms. Margaret became

ill some months before she died. Her youngest daughter, Penny, dreamed that her mother came and asked for permission to go on her way if she needed to do so. Penny said: 'No, you do *not* have my permission. I need you here!' She woke up very upset by the dream, for at that time no one realized how very ill Margaret was.

Six months later Margaret was in a coma. Penny sat at her bedside, held her hand, stroked her hair and suddenly remembered her dream. After much thought and many tears she said to her mother, 'I love you very much. I don't *want* you to leave – but yes, you have my permission to go.' Within ten minutes Margaret stopped breathing. Penny told me that, although she was unaware of it at the time, the dream had started to prepare her unconsciously for her mother's death. She was extremely upset even so, but by helping her mother in this way she was able to come to terms with this death.

Other Forms of Death Dream

This does not mean to imply that every death dream is a prediction of an actual death. It usually means that we must die to – let go of – the particular quality that in that moment the person we dream of represents. If I am particularly insecure, insanely jealous or constantly angry, I may dream of someone I know, who has the same problem, being run over by a ten-ton truck or falling off a cliff. It does not mean it is literally going to happen. Even if it does, we must still always look at what the person represents to us, and what we ourselves are meant to learn from it.

Death dreams can also help us make peace with someone after they have gone. I was speaking about this in a crystal workshop when discussing the qualities of rutilated quartz. Full of tiny gold or silver threads, it is a wonderful stone for keeping in touch with families and friends who are far away, dead and gone, or even to use as a link to past and future lives. The threads act like lines of connection and communication.

Dominic, suffering from unresolved problems with his alcoholic father who had died twenty years before, borrowed my rutilated quartz for the night and invoked a dream by which he could heal this relationship. It was almost as if he had called his father on the telephone, so instant was the response. In the dream his father explained to him why his life had been as it was, and that Dominic was in no way to blame. Father and son expressed love and forgiveness to each other, and later Dominic realized that he had always feared being the cause of his father's problems.

We can use dreams to heal many unresolved issues. The dream response may not always come as quickly as it did for Dominic; but if we persevere, come it certainly will.

Near-death experiences

So many of us in the West fear death, which is in fact as much a part of life as is birth. Death *is* a birth into another reality somewhere else; similarly, our birth here has been preceded by a death elsewhere. We came here as visitors, not to take up permanent residence.

We can invoke dreams to help us prepare for death, and free ourselves from this fear which also restricts life. In fact, dreams help us to adjust to this world by providing a bridge or lifeline to the next. When Plato was on his deathbed he was asked what was the most important message he wanted to leave behind for humanity. He replied: 'Practise to die.'

When talking to children about death I have often used the analogy of deep-sea diving. To go down into the sea you have to put on a wet-suit, flippers, goggles and a compressed-air tank. When we come out, all this gets in the way and has to be removed. In the same way we take off our bodies at death because we no longer need them. Children can be far more practical than adults about death, once they understand it properly.

Much of my own fear of death was alleviated through an NDE – a near-death experience – in which I left my body and floated above it before drifting down a deep blue tunnel in which someone reminded me I had not finished what I had come to do. Like many people who have had similar experiences, I found it incredibly free and exhilarating to be out of my body. Astral travel gives the same sense of freedom and reminds us that we are not just our body, which also releases the fear of death. Most of the indigenous dreamers with whom I have talked believe that we all explore astral realms when we sleep and dream.

Astral Travel

We all astral travel in dreams, whether we are aware of it or not.

There are two astral levels, instinctual and altruistic. The instinctual is close to the physical and ruled by emotion and desire. The altruistic is on a higher level of emotion; instead of self-gratification, it reaches out and cares for others. The astral body is an exact ethereal counterpart of a person's perfect physical body. In other words, if we are missing an arm or a leg, the astral body will not show it as lacking.

The astral body of a dying person can often be seen near the physical body, or even far away if there is a strong desire to see someone before death. The stronger the desire, the greater the ability to project the astral body. Many people have been visited in this way by a son, husband or lover killed in battle long before they received the official news. Anwar, the father of my Egyptian school friend, had an experience of this nature. When he was twenty-five his grandmother, unbeknown to him, was dying. She appeared in his room and smiled at him. He said she seemed to 'hang in the air' two or three feet off the floor, and was completely recognizable, but seemed much younger. He was in England at the time. About ten minutes after her 'visit' his parents telephoned him from Egypt to tell him that she was dead. My own great-aunt used to dash about London and visit Harrods in her astral body long after her physical legs refused to take her there!

Many people experience involuntary astral travel when they suddenly find themselves detached from their physical body through a sudden shock, anaesthesia, drugs or, of course, dreams. There is normally a sense of awareness of the physical body, to which the person is connected by what is known as the silver cord – a long, filmy cord that is broken at death. If during sleep we travel too far the cord can sometimes tighten and pull us back with such a jolt that we are literally jerked into our sleeping body, and awake feeling shocked and nauseated. This is different from a dream of falling from which we also suddenly wake up before we hit rock bottom, but without quite the same feeling of shock to the whole physical system.

Although at death a break in the silver cord takes place which is supposed to be irrevocable, I know a man who, after hearing himself being pronounced dead in hospital, found that his cord was still intact and so broke it apart himself. He floated about bodilessly quite happily, meeting deceased friends, but three days later found himself sucked willy-nilly back into his body. He was quite upset, but not nearly as upset as the morgue attendant, who fainted when he saw his supposedly dead client sit up under a sheet on a trolley!

Out-of-body experiences (OBEs)

After my own NDE, which happened spontaneously, I was determined to learn how to leave my body at will. I knew that it was part of the teaching in the ancient mystery schools, and that all shamans, magicians, occultists and medicine men practised it. So when I saw an advertisement in a local newspaper which asked 'Do you want to leave your body?', I answered it at once. Fifty of us spent three days sitting in chairs with our physical feet on the floor while the rest was supposed to be flying hither and thither to places and people we felt drawn to, while the group leader tapped on a glass. It worked for everyone there except me. They all had amazing out-of-body tales to tell, but all

I could say was that I felt a draught around my ankles and a pain in my head. I returned home, angry, frustrated, and convinced that there was something drastically wrong with me.

Following the class instructions, I tried daily to imagine jumping out of my body, or peeling it off like a wet-suit. Six months later nothing had happened. I decided I did not care any more, and threw myself on to my bed in anger and frustration.

Suddenly, without even trying, fully conscious – not drugged, drunk or sick – I found myself standing outside my body. I was so excited that I had no control over myself, and whirled madly around the room. Before I could think further I flew through the wall of my apartment and, after flying along streets about six feet off the ground, I entered a supermarket where I zoomed between ground-level shelves of potatoes, carrots and onions and five-feet-high shelves of champagne. Although I had no proper control and whizzed about at high speed, I was aware that I must confirm my experience, so I looked at names, prices and the faces of the checkout staff. As I whirled about I floated through trolleys – which normally ran mercilessly over my physical toes – and even the people shopping, until I was flying outside again, noting street names so that I could verify where I had been.

About thirty minutes after leaving my body I flew back through my bedroom walls. I was totally clear and objective, and immediately wrote down every detail of what had happened. I then went out and drove through the streets I had flown over – many of which I had not previously known. I found the supermarket, which I had never seen or been into before, and identified every single moment of my experience.

After this I had many out-of-body experiences. None of them was 'spiritual' – in the sense that I did not find myself at the feet of the Dalai Lama, nor making obeisance to a guru-hermit in a faraway Indian cave. I did move from Australia to England, then to America and to Europe, at the speed of light, and I did have an expansion of consciousness that enabled me to do, see and know things I could not have done with my physical senses.

After many happy OBEs something so frightening happened that I was shocked into realizing that I was here to be *in* my body and not out of it. I came back to Australia from an early morning jaunt to London and found I was back in my body but upside down. I was seeing the world around me through my feet. I have never felt such total fear and panic. For ten minutes I gazed at my upside-down apartment, wondering what to do. I could call a doctor or a psychiatrist, or commit suicide – but when you are looking at life through your feet everything seems impossible. If I had not known that suicide did not solve anything (because we only have to face the same challenges again), it would have been my first option. I suddenly felt very sad that I had not appreciated my body more, nor looked, listened, touched, felt and tasted life to the utmost degree. In the midst of despair I heard laughter fill the room and felt enormous pain in my intestines, as if a giant wooden spoon had stirred them. Suddenly I was no longer back to front or upside-down. Trembling with relief, I could see with my physical eyes again.

I decided to leave such journeys to my dreams, or to when I no longer had a physical body to return to. However, these experiences reinforced my absolute belief in the survival of my consciousness outside my body. I have a number of blind, paralysed or bedridden friends who frequently use astral travel to move beyond the restrictions imposed by their physical disabilities, and other friends who have learnt to project their astral bodies as a form of spiritual development. It was a commonplace skill in the past, and I'm sure will be one again in the future. In America a number of laboratories are conducting out-of-body research experiments, the best known being that of Robert Monroe in Virginia.

The basic requirement for astral travel is the belief that it is possible. The second is the will to do it. In my own case, the harder I tried the harder it became. Yet when, after months of trying, I relaxed and let it go, it happened almost by itself. I believe this is true of virtually anything we want to learn. We must practise endlessly until it becomes almost second nature, and then relax, so that our unconscious takes over and does it for us. Deep relaxation, in which we move away from being aware of our own bodies, visualization and meditation can help trigger OBEs or astral travel. To lie down and imagine a shadowy other self lifting or rolling out of the body, then to imagine it moving left and right and up to the ceiling, can also help detach the astral body from its physical counterpart.

In the Carlos Castenada books, Castenada was taught by his Yaqui teacher Don Juan how to astral travel while dreaming; and in *The Projection of the Astral Body*, written in 1929 by Sylvan Muldoon and Hereward Carrington, a doctor and specialist in psychic research, Muldoon suggests that to induce astral travel in dreams we should imagine going up in a lift to the top of a very high building as we lie down to sleep. Astral travel, whether consciously or unconsciously practised, prepares us for other worlds – worlds that dreams themselves introduce us to. Many historical accounts of astral travel describe the presence of a guiding friend and helper, and I would suggest that we too invoke a presence of help and protection before attempting this practice.

UFOs

At the same time that I experimented with astral travel or OBE, many of my friends were fascinated with UFOs – unidentified flying objects. In New York, I met a woman named Nancy, who told me the following story. She and three friends were on holiday. While watching the sunset from a local beauty spot, they saw a light coming out of the sky towards them. Thinking that it was an electrical storm they sat, watched and waited. After enjoying some spectacular explosions of almost rainbow-coloured lights, they decided it was time to go to bed.

Arriving back at the caravan park where they had arranged to spend the night, they discovered that three days and nights had passed since they had checked in. In panic Nancy telephoned her boyfriend in New York, who, thinking that the girls must have taken drugs, told them to go to the nearest hospital where he would pick them up. The hospital made no sense of their story, but discovered that small square patches of their hair had been removed from the back of their heads, and also believed that they were drugged.

Back in New York, Nancy's life changed. She read people's thoughts, saw auras and predicted the future. Life became increasingly difficult and her boyfriend, who refused to accept her story, left her for someone else. She then dreamed of a voice saying to her: 'We're very sorry to have caused you any harm. We're now going to terminate the experiment.' When Nancy woke up she could no longer see auras or predict people's thoughts, and at the back of her head there was a second patch of hair missing.

Chris was eight years old when, on his way home from school, he saw a UFO hovering over his small town. He said everything seemed to stop. There wasn't a breath of wind, not a leaf rustled on a tree, and even the milkman seemed transfixed with a milk bottle in his hand – 'and I felt as if my feet were glued to the pavement'. To this day, Chris has no idea how long this lasted. When he ran home to tell his parents about it they told him to get on with his homework and not to tell lies. Fortunately for Chris many people had reported the occurrence to the police, so he was vindicated.

He later joined a group who were trying to research UFO phenomena, and for the next ten years he dreamed every night that a woman spoke to him from another planet, reminding him of his real identity which, according to her, was not of this earth. As a result of the lessons she taught Chris his school work improved, and by the time I met him he had established himself as a successful poet-musician-storyteller. In fact his work had an uncanny beauty that sent chills up the spine.

Until he was eighteen he lived for his dreams. On his eighteenth birthday the woman told him that he was too involved with her and that it was unhealthy. 'You must live your own life on earth, and we must now cut the contact.' Chris was devastated, but she never returned. He too found a patch of hair missing, which has never regrown.

An analyst may say that Chris's dreams were an unconscious anima projection, and maybe they were. However, as a result of them he has been inspired to produce a wealth of wonderful music and words which in turn have inspired others. Nancy and Chris have never met, and each knows nothing of each other's stories, which took place many years and thousands of miles apart. Yet each had a square patch of hair removed – as did Nancy's friends. Whether we believe in UFOs as manifestations of extra-terrestrial intelligence, or prefer Jung's explanation that the UFO is a 'projection of a psychic content of wholeness often symbolized by a circle', there is no doubt that UFO sightings and contacts are becoming increasingly common both in and out of dreams.

10

HOW TO MAKE THE BEST USE OF YOUR DREAMS

I am sure that there are some simple secrets, some methods that can be learned, means of which we may in some measure command our dreams, and that more than we yet realize the control of our dreams lies in our power.

MARY ARNOLD-FOSTER, *STUDIES IN DREAMS*, 1921

Preparing for Sleep

One of the simplest ways we can begin to use this power is by preparing ourselves carefully for sleep. Most of us fall into bed at the end of a long, hard day, only to toss and turn, searching for relaxation of body and mind. We could use the time far better, sleep more deeply and dream more productively, if we did a little groundwork first.

If we did no more than mentally honour the night, sleep and dreams, as we got into bed, already the quality of our sleep and dreaming would improve. However, the more effort we put into pre-sleep rites, the more we impress our unconscious, sub-conscious and higher conscious selves that we are serious about dreams, and value the information they contain. Automatically our dreams will reflect this attitude – just as you or I will speak volumes to someone who listens, but will drop silent if he or she turns his head away each time we utter a word.

Most of us are not very good listeners. We listen with our mouths open to say what we want to say, rather than listen with our ears and minds open to take in what the speaker is saying. To be a good listener we need to empty ourselves of our own opinions and prejudices. It is exactly the same when going to sleep: we need to become empty and receptive. We are going to sit at the feet of a master teacher who can help us sort out and understand every aspect of life. Awake, we would not inflict our own ideas on such a person. We would listen expectantly, hoping to learn what we did not yet know. Many years ago the renowned spiritual teacher Krishnamurti attended a lecture given by a junior colleague who panicked when he saw the great man enter the room. He went to him and said: 'Sir, I cannot speak in front of you. Your wisdom is too great.'

Krishnamurti replied: 'I dropped everything I know outside the door. I am empty of all knowledge.'

For us to become empty before sleep means to let go of the day and everything that went on during it. One way of doing this is to sum up the day in your head – give it a title, good, bad, or indifferent, and either write it down or mentally release it as if you were letting a balloon float up into the sky. If you have a crystal, breathe the day into it, together with any problems you want to dispose of. The crystal technique is wonderfully healing, but don't forget to cleanse the crystal afterwards: either breathe the thought of light and love into it, or hold it under running water. In both cases, mentally affirm: 'I cleanse this crystal of all negativity' (or 'of anything not of itself').

No matter what went on in the day, or what you or anyone else did or did not do, try not to carry the day into the night. A very simple but effective affirmation to use, if there is a need to forgive, is this: 'Through the divine in me I forgive the human – in me *or* the other person.' It means I am involving a part of me beyond personality that *can* forgive, even when I find it difficult.

These techniques take very little time and can make a big difference not only to our sleep but also to our health. Even better is to keep a journal in which to record day-to-day events, the lessons we believe we are meant to learn from them, the people who made an impression on us (good or bad), recurring incidents (which mean that we are not learning the lessons), dreams, meditations and general insights. Because our dreams reflect our waking lives and a journal records them, a journal can be a powerful tool for dream interpretation as well as for releasing what is past.

Dreams and dream interpretation affect us physically, mentally, emotionally and spiritually. Consequently, preparation for sleep and dreams must include body, mind, feelings and spirit. Here are some of the most productive steps you can take:

1. Create a peaceful atmosphere in which you will feel comfortable and relaxed. For example, you can fill the bedroom with light and bright colours, crystals, candles, music, flowers and incense.

2. A wonderful way of releasing the past and relaxing is to soak in a hot ginger bath. Put two heaped tablespoons of powdered dry ginger in water as hot as your body can stand. Soak in it as long as you possibly can, then wrap up in a warm towel or blanket and go straight to bed. The ginger cleanses the auric field – the measurable electrical field around our bodies – and pulls out tension from muscles, cells and tissues. This is a powerful treatment, and should not be done every night, nor in the mornings.

3. Another effective way of releasing the day is to sit with your feet in a bowl of warm water and imagine your day draining out of your feet into the water. Back this up by breathing deeply throughout. As an alternative or refinement to this method, find a partner who will massage your feet with warm oil.

4. Dream pillows and special herbs can also help induce deep sleep and dreams. A dream pillow should be made of cotton or silk, fairly flat, and not more than fifteen by twelve inches. Among many recipes, one highly effective one mixes together one part rosemary, lavender and sweet marjoran and half a part thyme and spearmint. Then add one tablespoon of orris root powder, one tablespoon of dried orange peel and one teaspoon of powdered cinnamon. Mix well and put in the bag, which must be placed under the

pillow and slightly to one side so that the warmth from the sleeper's head causes the herbs to exude their fragrance and induce a sound natural sleep. Sage or camomile tea are both soothing pre-sleep drinks. One recipe for a tissane uses half a tablespoon of fresh or dried rosemary mixed with one and a quarter cups of cold water, brought to the boil and sweetened with honey.

5. Crystals are excellent catalysts both for dreaming and for helping you remember your dreams. Put them under the pillow, on a bedside table, on the floor or in the bed. The clearer and more sparkling a crystal is, the more stimulating it will be. The more opaque it is, the more calming and soothing its effect will be.

    Amethyst, rose quartz and blue lace agate are good to sleep with if you are under stress. Moonstone and selenite, two gems associated with the moon, contain within them the moon's power to give visions, including those in dreams. The moonstone is associated with the goddess Diana, and legends say that its brightness increases as the new moon becomes full. Opals and pearls are both moon and water gems. The opal is a gem of psychic awareness and can stimulate emotion in dreams. The pearl grows as the result of irritation, and can help us transmute and overcome our own negativity. Luvulite (or sugalite as it is sometimes called) and sodalite both help to open our Third Eye – the chakra or energy point in the centre of the forehead – and stimulate intuition and imagination – the dreaming side of the brain. Rutilated quartz helps to connect past, present and future, both in and out of dreams.

    Any of these gems can be placed in water and left out to absorb the moon's rays overnight. To drink moon-energized water before sleep is a delightful way to enhance dreaming.

6. To obtain best results in both sleep and dreaming, set the head of your bed towards magnetic north. This helps to balance the body and its etheric meridians – the lines of energy in our invisible body.

7. Always make sure that you have beside your bed a pen or pencil and a notebook, or else a tape recorder, plus a torch, in order to record your dreams promptly and accurately. Though a tape recorder is often easier to use, writing down a dream impresses it more deeply on the consciousness; by the act of writing, you have made the invisible visible. It is helpful also to keep an Ephemeris (an astrological table or calendar) beside the bed, to check the zodiac signs in which the moon is active, because the moon's phases affect dreaming.

8. Relaxing the body is a major element in all preparation for sleep, and among the most important methods is control of your breathing. Breathing in to the count of four, holding your breath for the count of four, then exhaling to the count of four, is an initial step in breath control. Any such disciplined breathing relaxes the body but stimulates the brain, which in turn stimulates the capacity for dreaming.

The most powerful technique that I know to stimulate relaxation, sleep and dreams is this. I kneel-sit back on my haunches, with both hands resting, palms up, on my knees. My eyes close, I inhale to the count of six, hold down in my diaphragm for six, then exhale to the count of six. I do this sequence at least six times – although it can be done for as long as you like. Still with my eyes closed, I touch the tip of my little finger to the tip of my thumb on each hand, while keeping the same rhythm of breathing. I then extend my little fingers and thumbs, while folding the three middle fingers of each hand into the palms. Then I close all the fingers over the thumb on each hand. Finally I go back to the starting position of my hands fully open on my knees.

This whole exercise induces deep relaxation, even if for any reason you are in great pain. You can still do it if you are lying on your back in bed, with your arms beside your body and your hands open palm upwards, or even if simply seated in a chair. The movements of the fingers alter when the breath goes into the lungs. This exercise is invaluable for anyone not able to move about freely, and for people in pain.

9. Another easy way to relax the body is to tense each muscle one by one, breathe in to the tensing movement and exhale sharply as you let go. For example, start with your left foot, leg and thigh. Tighten it all the way up, hold the tension for a moment, let go. Move to the right leg, stomach, buttocks, chest, left arm, right arm, back, shoulders, neck and so on up to the head and face, where you can grit your teeth and open your mouth wide as if to scream or yawn. This exercise can be done when you are sitting or lying down. Follow it by imagining light flowing into the top of your head and bathing every part of your body from top to toe. Think of the cells, organs and systems of the body renewed and revitalized. This exercise relaxes body and mind and is excellent for health, as is massage.

10. A dream is a psychic reading from our own personal Akashic record – the record of all our past lives. In order to be a clear channel unaffected by personality a good psychic will, before reading for a client, attune both to God and to the highest level of consciousness within him or herself and the client. It therefore makes good sense to attune yourself in the same way before sleep.

    This can be done through prayer, meditation, chanting (you can do this in the bath), or saying or singing a Mantram (words or sounds that induce a different level of consciousness) or the Om. The prayer or Mantram can be your own words, and could include asking for help, protection and guidance while asleep. Even to say no more than: 'I am doing this to get in touch with the highest within me' is enough to direct your conscious self to soul-level wisdom. Twenty to thirty minutes' meditation before sleep, or when you wake up, can provide as much benefit as three to four hours' sleep.

11. Before turning out the light do not forget to write down: 'I want to dream and I want to remember my dreams.' This programmes your dreaming self to respond, and could also be used as an affirmation before sleep. If there is a particular

subject or problem about which you need information or greater clarity, write that down too. Remember that to ask a dream for help, healing or insight is dream incubation, and it will work better if you immerse yourself in the subject first, as well as concentrate on it before sleep. If you want to fly or astral travel in a dream, watch birds and planes and study the mechanics of flying and imagine you too can lift off. You can also programme a crystal to stimulate clear dream answers. Breathe the thought of what you need into the crystal while holding it in your right hand, and then put it under your pillow. A crystal, whether programmed or not, still stimulates dreaming, but in this way it lends extra energy to the subject in hand.

12. Once you are in bed with the lights out there are any number of imaginative exercises which induce deep sleep and more profound dreams. For example, you can visualize being inside a five-pointed star (the sign of the perfected man, and therefore a good shape within which to sleep) or surrounded by emerald-green light, a beautiful garden, a temple or any kind of special place you have created with your imagination that provides a sanctuary or sacred space within which dreams can unfold. The main point to remember is that all visualization techniques slow the brainwave rhythm to Alpha, and therefore help pre-sleep relaxation.

If you find it difficult to visualize, counting backwards from twenty-one to zero is another way of lowering the brain into Alpha. Remember, too, that thinking of places and events in which you are happy, like dancing with your lover or walking in a garden, can be as effective as a 'formal' visualization. Before sleep I often imagine myself inside a crystal, or inside a room in which I am bathed with colour, or on top of a snow-covered mountain in Tibet, or inside a temple of healing or learning. You might like to imagine drifting away in a hot-air balloon or sliding down rainbows – let yourself go anywhere that your imagination wants to take you. The more creative you are before sleep, the more colourful and enjoyable your dreams are likely to be.

Imagine meeting your dream guide or teacher, who will not only help you dream but will also help you understand your dreams.

13. A very effective dream trigger is to put a glass of water next to the bed and to drink half of it just before sleep, affirming: 'I *will* dream and I *will* remember my dream.' Immediately you wake up in the morning you should drink the other half of the glass and repeat the affirmation. This helps to fix the idea of dreaming in your mental computer, which like any other computer gives out what we have put into it once it has accepted the message.

Most people dream less if they are very tired and under a lot of emotional stress. Sleeping pills, drugs and alcohol can also interfere with your ability to dream. If you have never concentrated on dreaming before you may need to be both patient and persistent to achieve results, but these can well prove richly rewarding.

Although this long list of pre-sleep instructions may look daunting, all the techniques are simple, bring results, and do not take a lot of time. When you first do them you may have to stretch yourself a little, but if, over time, you try them all, you will probably find one or two that work for you better than the others. You may also want to adapt or develop them to your own needs. What is important is that you discover what works for you. Exploration of our inner worlds through the magic mirror of dreams needs to be fun. Expect to sleep and dream with joy, pleasure and delight, and you will.

Remembering Your Dreams

After sleep, many of us forget our dreams because we are woken up by children or an early-morning alarm, or by getting out of bed too quickly. Pre-sleep preparation helps to cure that.

1. If, in spite of trying out the recommendations above, you still find it difficult to remember your dreams, you may find taking niacin and large doses of vitamin B6 – the 'mental vitamin' – helpful. A shortage of B6 makes it difficult to remember dreams. To spend five or ten minutes visualizing yourself going to sleep, dreaming, and writing the dream down when awake is often enough to trigger a satisfactory response. If you wake naturally during the night, always write down whatever you can recall of your dreams. If you don't wake naturally, a more drastic solution is to set an alarm clock to wake you every ninety minutes. Then immediately write down everything you can remember. Although this course of action may be unpopular if you have a non-dreaming sleeping partner it works within two or three days, and is usually needed only once.

2. The first step in dream recall for most people is to try and wake up slowly. If the memory of the dream is clear and strong, keep still and, with eyes closed, re-experience it by allowing the dream and its images to float through your mind before writing them down.

3. If you wake up with a huge dream scenario that vanishes into thin air as you reach for your pad, relax back into the bed, close your eyes, breathe deeply and then roll over into a different position. If the dream does not come back, think backwards. For example, what was going on in your mind before you opened your eyes? What were you feeling when you went to bed? What did you write in your journal before sleep? What did you do yesterday? This can help the memory click back into the dream.

4. Even if you cannot remember a dream, *always write something down* – a fragment of a dream, a colour, a symbol, the feeling or thought you wake up with. These thoughts often come from the night's dreams and may be the first clues to retrieving them.

5. If absolutely nothing comes to mind, take a few deep breaths, count from ten to zero, pick up your pen and start to write without thinking. Don't judge it – just keep the pen moving and let the pen do the thinking. This is another way of encouraging the unconscious to speak, which Edgar Cayce called inspirational writing. It is a method that aligns you with your own dream-producing self, and the result may be a story, a comment or just meandering words. You can use all or any part of this exactly as you would a dream, and with practice it can become a powerful source of information.

6. When recording a dream, note important symbols such as numbers, words, figures of speech, puns or names first, and do not try to analyse or interpret the dream while writing it down. (Plays on words, or an abstract idea expressed in a more literal form, often crop up in dreams. For instance, one woman dreamed, during a period of emotional frigidity after an unhappy divorce, that she was trapped in Iceland. The dream was repeated until she took steps to free her emotional self from its frozen condition.)

7. Describe, in as few words as possible, your feelings, thoughts and insights about the dream, as well as your physical reactions to it. Remember the people, objects and events, and what they mean to you.

8. Take one part of your dream at a time and use your imagination to be in it. *Listen* to your dream before trying to interpret it.

9. Realize your dream, or bring its energy into the day by acting it out. Do this by contacting the people you dreamed of, wearing clothes of the same colour that you dreamed of, and using the same objects – like your car, your favourite armchair or your desk at work. For example, I once awoke with a fragment of dream in which I was planting seeds in the earth. Later that day I in fact planted some small seed-

lings in my garden, and immediately remembered the rest of the dream. The unconscious often prefers its own moment to emerge, and by bringing the dream into the day we give it an importance which encourages it to emerge more easily.

10. One level of the unconscious contains numerous temporarily obscured thoughts and impressions that affect both dreams and waking life. Jung described this level as a little like a car around a corner, out of sight but still there. The unconscious can sometimes behave rather like a very shy or wild animal that needs to be tamed and trained before it will show itself. Consciousness often resists what is hidden and unknown in the unconscious, and needs help in dropping its barriers of judgement, prejudice, opinions and preconceived notions. Art, music, acting, dance, movement, drawing, painting, writing, sculpture, even exercise – in fact any kind of creative activity – all help the consciousness to let go and the unconsciousness to rise to the surface.

11. Another excellent way to recall and record a dream is to draw or paint it in a circle. The circle mediates between left and right brain, conscious and unconscious, and symbolizes the whole self. When used in this way it can be a powerful tool for revealing stages of your life, as well as your physical, mental, emotional and spiritual health. Before going to sleep draw a circle and put your art materials near your bed. When you wake up, reach for whichever colours feel most appropriate and quickly put into the circle the symbol, feeling or image that connects you to the dream. This could be a blob of colour, a flower or a rainbow – it does not have to be a drawing of each item in the dream; it is simply a way to register the feeling. If you have forgotten the dream, this will usually jog your memory. If you record your dreams this way, over time you will have a series of Mandalas that can give enormous insight into both waking and dreaming life. Used as a focus for reflection or meditation, they can awaken a depth of awareness you never knew you had.

12. Dream recall is easier at dawn. This is an especially sacred and creative time, when inner and outer worlds blend.

13. Meditation on a dream, even when you cannot remember it, can sometimes bring it back. To have faith and trust that whatever the dream is saying is exactly what you need to hear at the moment will also help you absorb the dream's message, even if you do not remember the dream.

14. Meet your dream guide or teacher and ask him or her to reveal the dream and its message to you. To do this, imagine going through a door and down steps which lead you to a beautiful garden. Make it so real that you can almost smell the grass and flowers, feel the breeze in your hair and the warmth of the sun on your cheeks, hear the rustle of leaves in the trees, the trickle of water from a pool or stream, and see clouds drifting lazily overhead. Your dream guide is waiting for you, maybe under a tree or paddling in the stream. You can ask any questions you want about the dream and its meaning – or even ask to have the dream rerun like an old movie. I have successfully used this method or variations of it hundreds of times in workshops, including with people who could not recall their dreams. You can also make a tape for yourself with similar suggestions, and play it back. To be more effective, breathe deeply, count down from ten to zero, and relax the body first.

15. During the day your dream may suddenly reappear. Try to jot down the most important symbols and impressions and, if you can, re-experience them and actualize them (see 9, above).

16. When re-experiencing the dream, question the people, animals, objects and symbols in it. Be patient: allow them to speak and answer you. By doing this you give them life and receive wisdom in return.

17. Reread your dreams, and give each one a title which sums

up its essence, so that in two months you can immediately recall the 'Bicycling Elephant' or the 'Woman with Green Hair' dreams. If you keep a dream journal you will begin to see an emerging pattern of progress or recurring events – dreams studied in a series give more insight than when looked at individually.

18. Do not be afraid of anything that the unconscious wishes to share; there is nothing in the unconscious which is not already in life. The unconscious will often exaggerate a message to impress it more emphatically on our waking consciousness. The more we dialogue with and open ourselves to the unconscious, the more clear and simple these messages will become.

19. Dream recall is an acquired habit, and can be learnt. To write: 'I want to dream, remember and understand my dreams' implies 'I'm ready to listen.' It is an invitation to speak that our inner selves have probably been waiting a lifetime to receive, and therefore an opportunity that will not be refused.

20. Dream recall requires faith, devotion and humility: faith that dreams are important, devotion to dreams and to making them a living reality by incorporating them into life, and humility to recognize that something greater than personality is working through you.

    For shamans, magicians and indigenous peoples the world of dreams is a psychic reality with a dynamic, an energy as real as life itself. Interaction with this world of dreams leads to their greater understanding of their waking world, and so it can for us too. Dreams are an open road to creativity, change and self-understanding. Initially to follow some of the pre-sleep and dream recall suggestions may mean getting up a little earlier or going to bed a little later, but you will find you need less sleep, you feel great, and your increased awareness will affect everyone around you positively.

Dreams operate on many levels at once and, like the Mandala or circle, mediate between the left and right brain, conscious and unconscious, active and passive, positive and negative, Yin and Yang, male and female. Prayer and conversation are an outward expression of inner thoughts and feelings, and so use Yang or masculine energy. Meditation, listening, feeling and reflection are passive, receptive and otherwise feminine or Yin energy. In dreams we are both active and passive, sometimes witnessing ourselves, as if at a movie, and at other times performing in similar action-packed dramas. Dreams are a middle point of balance, barometers of our feelings and ambassadors of our souls. Dreams open us to possibilities of which we may not be aware when we are fully awake.

A dream is like an oracle that brings to life what has been hidden or only dimly felt. Although pre-sleep and dream recall techniques have great value, the only sure way of fully grasping the true meaning of a dream is by exploring it systematically as soon as possible after experiencing it. There are myriad ways of doing this.

Exploring Your Dreams

1. My favourite way of exploring a dream systematically is:
   (a) To give the dream a title which embodies its essence. When you do this, ask yourself: 'Will I remember this dream two years from now by recalling the title?' If you are not sure, change the title.
   (b) To describe the dream feelings – which may be hate, fear, love, apprehension, confidence or confusion. Include the sense of physical, mental, emotional, spiritual or psychic energy contained within the dream.
   (c) Outline the setting – is it 'man-made', meaning cars, buses, parking areas, houses, cities and so on, or 'natural', that is, meadows, gardens, forests, seas or streams.

(d) Note the people – remembering that each one reflects an aspect of your own personality.

(e) List the symbols and objects – especially those that in some way stand out. For example, the tiger in the back seat of the car, or the prickly cactus that replaces my husband in bed beside me.

(f) Sum up – in as few words as possible – what the dream means to you.

(g) Bring the dream to resolution by applying its meaning to your life.

To work with a dream in this way avoids writing down the whole dream story, while still bringing into sharp focus what is essential in the dream. It is *not* dream interpretation, but can give extraordinary insight into the dream's message.

Here is an example. I, Sophie, am in the driving seat of a car with no steering-wheel. My mother tries to direct from the back seat.

> *Title:* 'Out of Control'.
> *Feelings:* Fear, frustration, helplessness.
> *Setting:* Car, man-made.
> *People:* Mother and self.
> *Symbols/objects:* Car, missing steering-wheel.
> *Summary:*
>> *(i)* My mother is trying to control my life, or
>> *(ii)* I have abdicated my power to direct my life to that over-protective and over-caring aspect of my personality symbolized by my mother, or
>> *(iii)* I give my power to direct my life away to any dominant authority.
>
> *Resolution:* I shall take full control of my life, starting by moving out of the family home to my own flat, and finding a job and friends that satisfy the real me, rather than the authority-fearing side of me.

Sophie may not be able to do all this at once, but if she takes one step at a time – such as by wearing clothes that make her feel happy rather than respectable – she will begin to actualize her dream's message, and subsequently change her life.

2. Another very simple and effective way of working with a dream is to extract three major points from it, and describe in a word what they mean to you at that moment. For example, my husband may symbolize a lover one week and a beast the next, and my children joy, innocence and delight, or rebellious fiends. Write a sentence combining what these three major points mean to you, then reduce that sentence to one word and insert 'I am' before it. This method allows unknown feelings to come to the surface, from which you can create a positive affirmation of life. If a negative statement is created, we must reverse it – for example, from 'I am fear' to 'I am courage'. This method enables you to tap in to energies beyond the rational self which are uniquely helpful for fundamental change.

Here is how working on a dream by this method looks in practice. Ann dreamed that she found a red lacquer house, outside which was a greyhound track to which her son had become addicted – 'gone to the dogs'.

> *Ann's three major points:*
> (i) House – safety, comfort.
> (ii) Red lacquer – polish.
> (iii) Gone to the dogs – let go.
> *Ann's sentence:* I let go of comfort and polish to find new self.
> *Ann's single word:* I am fulfilled.

Tom, with the same dream, might assess it quite differently:
> *Tom's three major points:*
> (i) House – prison.
> (ii) Red lacquer – prostitutes, night life.
> (iii) Gone to the dogs – addiction to gambling.
> *Tom's sentence:* By my addiction to immorality I risk prison.
> *Tom's single word:* I am threatened.

As this is a negative statement, Tom must reverse it to pull the energy from the dream. It then becomes: I am absolved.

Harry dreamed that his mother poured water into a cup which overflowed no matter how fast he tried to drink it.

Harry's three major points:
  (i) Water – love.
  (ii) Cup – self.
  (iii) Overflowed – too much.
Harry's sentence: Too much love is overwhelming me.
Harry's single word: I am suffocated.
Reversal: I am free.

To create an affirmation or an ideal from a dream in this way brings the dream energy into the day, and is far more effective than any affirmation or ideal that you pick out of a book. The way to use your affirmation is to repeat it in your head as often as you can, which gives you secure space from which to step into the day. If things go wrong, by repeating your affirmation you call on the dream's energy and gain access to more profound and expert levels of yourself. You can use the same techniques to analyse your waking hours as if they too were a dream. By doing this you begin to understand yourself much better, as well as the hidden meaning that lies beneath the surface of everyday events. The more you can open the door to the unconscious, the clearer its messages will become.

3. Dream re-entry, where you close your eyes and re-experience the dream in order to understand it and bring it to completion if it is unfinished, is particularly useful when working with nightmares or recurring dreams. The Senoi system (see p. 87) lends itself well to dream re-entry:
   (a) To confront and conquer danger in a dream.
   (b) To advance towards pleasure, and
   (c) Always to obtain a positive outcome.

The system can transform the most terrifying dream image into something happy and acceptable.

Response (a), to confront and conquer danger, means never

running away but instead to face the threat. This means fighting, pointing a crystal, or direct a ray of light, colour or your own arm towards it. If necessary call on dream friends or authority figures to help, but remember you are the one who must confront the danger. If the threat is from an accident such as a car crash, or falling off a cliff, rather than from a person, re-experience it to see what happens. For example, imagine that you fall off the mountain, sink to the bottom of the sea, die in the car crash, or are sealed into the coffin. You will be amazed at what transpires, and how powerfully you can resurrect negative energy.

The Senoi system's *(b)*, to advance towards pleasure, means that you should enjoy dream friends as fully as possible, including sexually. Remember that sexual energy is creative, and creative energy is sexual. The unconscious does not distinguish between the two. The more sexual you are in dreams the more creative you will be in waking life. Dream lovers, even if disguised as Tom or Jane from next door, are aspects of yourself, so do not feel guilty.

The Senoi system's *(c)*, always to obtain a positive outcome, means that you should *demand* a gift from anyone who has threatened you, or *ask* politely for a gift from a friend, or *find* your own if no one else was involved.

Dream re-entry enables us to talk to the dream images, rewrite the dream story if we do not like it, carry the dream forward or backward, reclaim lost parts of ourselves and bring everything to completion. If you are very stuck with a dream it is helpful to have a friend guide you through the process. Remember not to censor anything that comes up. Dream re-entry and dream dialogue are similar to Jung's active imagination (p. 71), and allow the imaginative creative part of us to speak while we are fully conscious. Dream re-entry works better if you relax first – use any of the pre-sleep exercises described earlier. Finally, dream re-entry is a means of profound change, and even a fragment of dream is enough to work with.

4. Dream dialogue can involve talking to the whole dream or

just to parts of it. For example, ask your dream: 'What are you telling me? How are you healing me? Warning me? What part of me does X represent? What does X need from me? What action do you want me to take?' You may prefer to speak to X directly: 'What are you doing? How do you feel?' Let the answers float into your mind, and do not be put off by thoughts of 'I'm making this up.' It is coming from a real and inner part of you, expressed by your imagination.

Dream dialogue is not interpretation, but creates an opportunity to interact with our inner life, and can lead to great understanding of the self. Dream dialogue can also be done on paper through journal writing, or by listing the cast of characters and what they want to say. It is as if you were writing a script for a movie or play.

To show you how much can come from so little, Jon dreamed he tripped over a lump of coal. He imagined asking it what it was doing in his way, and it began to change into a squat little troll with a mop of black hair. When Jon said: 'Who are you?' the troll replied: 'You don't care, and I'm not going to tell you.'

Jon said: 'Look at me!' and the troll began to shrink. Desperate for some kind of dialogue, he imagined pushing away the troll's hair from its eyes. As he did so, he saw himself when he was three years old and he immediately remembered long hours spent locked in a coal cellar while his alcoholic father went on drunken rampages. Jon was now forty-five, and until this dream he had forgotten how frightened and abandoned he had felt for most of his childhood. This released such a flood of memory that Jon wept for half an hour, realizing too how inhibited he was as a result of his past. Finally, he imagined taking the troll by the hand and telling him he wanted to get to know him better. The troll immediately grew waist high and began to look quite human. This dream enabled Jon to cure his childhood traumas, and helped him to become more of an extrovert.

5. Similar to dream dialogue is the Gestalt method, developed by Fritz Perls, in which the dreamer starts off by retelling the

dream in the first person and present tense. This approach helps bring the dream and its emotions to life. The dreamer next takes the part of each dream image, and voices its message and states what it represents. This procedure uses chairs or cushions to symbolize each image, and the dreamer moves from one to the other to express its viewpoint and ask its questions.

For example, I dream I'm a child climbing a tree when a man with an axe comes to cut it down. I try to stop him, and wake up. As the child addressing the man, I might say: 'How can you spoil my fun? I play in this tree every day. Birds build their nests and squirrels hide their nuts in it. This tree is my friend. It's not fair to chop it down.' I now move to the chair symbolizing the man, and perhaps say: 'Winter's coming. We need wood for the fire, and you're too big to be climbing trees anyway.' I next represent the tree, when I might say: 'I'm part of the family and I shelter many living things. I'd not mind being cut down if I were to be turned into useful and beautiful furniture, but *not* if I'm just to be burnt in a fire.' The dreamer goes on with this role-playing until the dream's full meaning is uncovered.

What is especially useful with this method is that it enables us to discover how we see ourselves and others, if our needs are being met, what our conflicts are, and how we should negotiate with different qualities and feelings (the weak or bossy part, or the animus and anima, or the child and the parent). Gestalt is as applicable to waking life as to dreams, and can give us incredible understanding of other people by allowing us temporarily to 'become them'.

6. Art and dreams: some dreams have strong images, others strong feelings. Pick an image or feeling that in some way speaks to you more than anything else in the dream, and then draw or paint the essence of it. You do not need to draw an exact picture, and you may prefer to use clay to sculpt it, or to gather flowers, twigs, leaves and stones and create it in another way, or to make a collage out of fabric or pictures from a magazine. You should use what

is the most natural and easiest thing for you to handle.

Once you have completed your picture, study it – immerse yourself in it. Imagine talking to it, being inside it, feeling its energy and the effect of its colours. If it could speak to you, what would it say? As in a dream dialogue, allow any thoughts, words, feelings and insights to float to the surface, without judging them. Any strong symbol or feeling can be the foundation for this kind of creation, which brings the emotion out of the depths of our psyche, and clarifies what might otherwise only have been dimly felt. Meditate on it, leave it around where you can see it easily and often. Draw or create it again in a few weeks, and see if it has changed in any way. You are allowing aspects of yourself to express themselves in a way that may have been blocked before, so do not force yourself to find meaning until it is ready to come. This kind of exercise helps to develop our creativity, and assists us in accepting that our inner selves are as much a part of us as walking, talking, thinking and listening.

Out of dozens of dreamwork methods, the ones I have described here are those which I have successfully used myself over many years. They work as well with groups as with individuals. No matter how you work with a dream, always follow through on its message by incorporating it into your waking life. If it seems too big to do all at once, take a step at a time. If you cannot discover the message, simply enjoy the dream on its own merits.

Don't ignore your dreams

Once you feel you know what your dreams are trying to tell you, don't ignore their message. As a boy Paul was consistently top of the class. He then won a scholarship to university, and his delighted parents gave him a car as a reward. Twelve months later Paul was on the verge of expulsion for doing no work and failing his exams. Each parent tried to speak to him. His father said: 'Your mother is worried about you.' His mother said: 'Your father is worried about you.' His professor spoke to him. Paul shrugged them all off. These are all ways in which the inner self will try to communicate before it gives a dream message.

Paul now dreamed he was being chased up hill and down dale by his car, which had acquired enormous teeth. When his mother said: 'I think the dream is trying to tell you something', Paul ignored her. He was fed up with years of study and the car gave him a reason to stay out late with friends, have a good social life, take the engine apart and put it together again at weekends, and generally become an academic dropout. The dream told him that the energy he was putting into his car was threatening to devour him.

On some level Paul knew this, because he awoke shaking and sweating with fright as if from a nightmare. Nightmares are the demand for attention that wakes us from sleep into life – if we listen. If Paul had responded to the wisdom that tried to speak through the dream he might have said, 'OK, my work is poor. I know I'm spending too much time with the car, but I'm sick of all work and no play, so I'll use the week to study and the weekend to play.' Instead he dismissed the dream as crazy and went on as before. Ten days later his car was smashed to smithereens in an accident. Fortunately Paul walked away unhurt, and only then was he shocked into resuming his studies.

Practical Dream Interpretation

1. Dream interpretation can be simple. It can range from making an intuitive guess about what the dream means to a deep exploration of its every facet. Whatever you do, try to stay with what the dream means to *you*, and not what a dream dictionary or your best friend says. Do not try to force meaning on a symbol, or you will limit the interpretation. Symbols often have more than one meaning, and we need to explore them on different levels – physically, mentally, emotionally and spiritually.

    This is where Freud's free association can be useful. Write the dream down, and then add whatever words come spontaneously in association with what is in the dream. From one word such as 'tent' I might write down 'childhood, circus, animals, trapped, caged' and deduce that I am currently feeling as trapped as when I was a child. Dream symbols have an energy and meaning unique to the dreamer. When you click into what is the correct interpretation for you, it will resonate inside you.

2. Like dream recall, dream interpretation is easier early in the morning when our censoring ego's defences are down, and when we have woken up naturally without an alarm clock. Make an intuitive guess at the overall meaning of your dream, and also imagine what it might be telling you to do. Do not think too hard, and trust what comes into your mind. Remember what you were doing and feeling in the dream, and see if it reminds you of anything in outer life. Dreams reflect inner and outer reality, and if you keep a journal in which you record briefly the day's events, as well as your dreams, that will help you to interpret both.

3. The cast of characters in our dreams should always be interpreted first as aspects of ourselves, no matter what secondary meaning they might have. We must look for the quality in us that our dreams have chosen to disguise with the image of someone else. To note the people in our lives, and what they mean to us, can help clarify their presence in our dreams. To dream of people from the past, especially those we have been close to, can symbolize the characteristics we have taken on from them, whereas if we dream of people from the present that is usually saying how we ourselves feel about them. Whether looking at king, queen, president, movie star, bus conductor or your own child, look at *why* your unconscious has chosen to project that particular image on your dream screen. What is he or she doing, saying, feeling, and what is that telling you about you? Remember that names, too – such as Grace Seechrist, Mr Lord and Holly Wiseman – often contain a message.

4. Animals symbolize the animal or instinctive physical side of our nature, which can be wild or domesticated. To interpret animals, such as a playful kitten, a roaring lion or a gentle lamb, look at what they represent to you. The more wild a dream animal is, the more you are being shown that you are out of control – especially if it is chasing you. For six months Betty dreamed that she was being chased by a rampant tiger, before she realized that it symbolized her own bad temper and tendency to pounce on her family; the dream helped her to take charge of this habit and control it. Birds, although they can be both wild and domesticated, usually represent spirit, the ability to soar, to transcend earthliness and to move into higher levels of consciousness. Obviously a vulture is going to have a different meaning from a dove, and therefore the kind of bird it is, its activity and your association with it will all affect the interpretation.

5. Emotional dreams are usually more colourful and vivid, and therefore easier to remember; in fact, black and white dreams tend to be devoid of emotion. The elements – earth, air, water and fire – in a dream also play a part in its physical, mental, emotional and spiritual interpretation. Earth dreams often signify down-to-earth practicality, unless the earth is muddy, which can symbolize feeling debased or bogged down in something. Air represents the mind, and airy dreams usually suggest increased clarity and the influx of new ideas. On the other hand, if the air is turbulent, such as in a hurricane, storm or tornado, the dream may suggest mental turbulence which could cause further problems. A dream-teaching friend, who works with children, told me she dreams of tornadoes striking the houses of children who subsequently get into some kind of trouble. It has now become her early-warning system for children who need help.

Dreams in which water plays a significant part deal with our emotional states, although water can also represent spirit. If you are drowning, or lost in a small boat in a savage and thunderous sea, you are probably going through considerable emotional upheaval; whereas water that has dried up or frozen suggests that you are feeling emotionally dried up or frigid. Spiritual water might be symbolized by a pool or stream in which you immerse yourself, as if in baptism, or drink from a chalice. When Molly sees huge tidal waves engulfing either herself, her family or friends, she now knows that something drastic is going to happen that will affect the emotional stability of everyone involved in the dream. Fortunately, this helps her prepare rather than panic.

Fire dreams stimulate spiritual awareness, growth and warmth. To dream of being caught in a fire can imply a spiritual cleansing, a burning away of materialism, while to be struck by lightning can imply instant spiritual revelation.

6. Dreams with natural backgrounds such as landscapes, hills, valleys, mountains, deserts, forests, rivers, lakes, beaches and meadows tend to signify what I call soul level dreams – dreams of the true, natural self – whereas dreams of man-made cities, factories, airports, towns, houses, trains, cars, shops and stations tell us about the 'man-made' personality and its journey through life.

7. To dream of a child – taking care of or playing with it – generally signifies that you are in touch with the Christ child, or with the pure, innocent, holy part of yourself. Dreams of your own children can also represent innocence, as well as disobedience and rebellion. A child can also mean immaturity, or even your own lost inner child. If you dream of giving birth to a baby, you give birth to another level of consciousness. If you abandon it, the dream suggests that you refuse to take responsibility for higher wisdom. Dream research shows that pregnant women who dream of giving birth usually have a very easy labour.

8. The Holy Child – like the Wise Old Man, the Earth Mother, the Shadow, the Animus, the Anima, the God and Goddess, the Trickster and the Whore – is one of Jung's archetypal

figures common to all mankind, and will, like all the others, appear in our dreams from time to time. So too will archetypal themes such as death, loss and separation, or growth, love and marriage – which usually symbolizes union with the higher self. But no matter how universal the symbol may be, it is still, in the moment of the dream, a personal expression of the consciousness of the dreamer who dreams it. It is therefore uniquely individual as well as universal, and should be interpreted as such (see Chapter 11).

9. The best way to interpret your dreams is to learn your own dream language, and the best way of doing this is to watch your dreams and from them create your own dream dictionary. Note whether the dream came at the beginning, middle or end of your sleep. Research by the well-known clinical psychologist Dr Stanley Krippener shows that early-sleep dreams were to do with the past, middle-sleep dreams with the present, and dreams just before waking with the future. Record your own interpretations, note recurring dream themes, colours, numbers, symbols, people and what they mean to you. For instance, I am allergic to dairy products. If I dream of cheese I know that I am being told to change my diet, even if I have not in fact eaten any. Pat's mother died from a bee-sting, so that if Pat dreams of bees she knows that the dream is saying 'Watch out!', although she is not literally in life-threatening danger. In a dream workshop, a group of people imagined what it was like to be the road in Katie's dream. One person felt angry and abused by the endless stream of cars, carelessly using her to go wherever they wanted. Another felt delighted at being the means by which people and goods travelled about. Yet another saw the road as flattened, downtrodden and harassed. Each one perceived it differently, and each perception reflected an inner attitude, which is why it is so important for us to interpret our own dreams.

Dream symbols disguise feelings. Dream interpretation means translating the picture back to the feeling. It is not difficult to do this. By contemplating symbols you become one with them, and can then discover what they are and where they came from. To observe and contemplate outer life events can lead to similar discoveries.

Not everyone dreams in pictures. Wilma always dreamed in geometric shapes, although in waking life she was a talented artist. Geometric shapes and numbers are an expression of inner-level mental planes. They are often the sign of strong intuition, and can be contemplated the same way as any other symbol.

10. Rod Suskin, a South African astrologer and dream interpreter, suggests that an astrological chart can, to some extent, show the kind of symbolism likely to come up in someone's dreams, as well as the issues or concerns that may affect them. Suskin says that from the position of Neptune in the chart he has a road into the dream world of the dreamer, so perhaps adding an astrological chart to your dream dictionary will assist your interpretation.

11. A final suggestion to aid dream interpretation is before you go to sleep to visualize yourself first dreaming, and then interpreting the dreams. This fixes the idea of 'I *can* do it!' in your consciousness, and creates a backdrop, like a stage set, against which the dream can unfold. This exercise is usually more productive if you visualize this taking place within an enclosed space such as a cave, a glade surrounded by trees, a special dream house, temple or room, and can include meeting a dream guide or teacher. Do not be afraid to ask questions or to request a repeat of the dream until you fully understand its meaning.

To learn the language of dreams means to learn your own wisdom. Like learning any other language, it takes practice, persistence and humour. To learn to control your dreams means that you learn to take charge of your life, that you can rehearse new options and make new choices. To actualize your dream and bring its wisdom into the day – even if it is only to wear the colours of the dream – means that you are beginning to take responsibility for what you know. Remember that dreams try to show us what we do *not* know, rather than what we know already, so drop any theories about how a dream *should* be. No matter what interpretation you put on your dreams, they are only truly understood when they lead to change. Even if we do no more than think about dreams a little, they will inevitably begin to empower us to live life with greater freedom and happiness.

As George Bernard Shaw said:

> *Other people see things and say 'Why?'*
> *But I dream things and say 'Why not?'*

11

SYMBOLS AND COLOURS
IN DREAMS

I will speak in secret to my soul, and in friendly conversation I will ask her what I would like to know. No stranger shall be present, we will talk alone and openly to each other. Thus I need not be afraid to ask even the most secret things, and she will not be ashamed to reply honestly.

HUGH ST VICTOR

A dream is a secret conversation, an intimate communication from the soul to the personality, an encoded message unique to the dreamer. It is therefore illogical to imagine that dream symbols have exact and invariable meanings. A fire may mean warmth, family and love to one person, to another pain, death and destruction, while someone else again sees it as transformation, purification, or the positive destruction of the past for rebirth, similar to the Phoenix rising from the ashes. People who choose to interpret dreams from a general dream dictionary will tend to get stuck with a possible surface meaning of the dream, and thus miss the waking-life event which is usually the emotional trigger that underlies the dream's real message.

Only the dreamer knows the full meaning of his dream. Never rest exclusively on someone else's interpretation. Other people's insight may catalyse a deeper understanding, but it is coloured by their own experience, prejudice and perception.

Making Use of 'Signposts'

When working with a dream, note the important symbols, numbers, figures of speech, words, puns and names first. Sum up what you feel the dream is saying – its overall meaning for you and your life – and when you do so, re-experience this rather than analytically detach yourself from it. Look at what each image means by itself as well as within the dream. Pay attention to recurring dreams and symbols. Record major colours and symbols, and, after six months or more, see if there is a connection between a particular dream theme and a colour or symbol. Dreams respond to what occurs during the day; therefore look for the event that triggered the dream. Assess how your dream affects you physically, mentally, emotionally and spiritually.

Dream interpretation should be simple, practical, sensible and functional – helping us to improve our everyday lives, to opt *into* life rather than cut off from it. So no matter how universal dream symbols appear to be, they are in fact an exclusive expression of the person who dreams them, and should be interpreted as such. With this qualification, here is a range of meanings for a variety of symbols. This guide is compiled from my own dream experience and that of other people whose dreams I have investigated. If these meanings 'fit', you will know; otherwise use them as a key for general guidance only.

Symbols

AEROPLANE   Expansion. Elevated consciousness. Ability to 'fly high'.

AIR   Freedom, breath of life.

ALCOHOL   Denial of self, of life. Escape, illusion, giving away power.

ANGEL   Protection, guidance, love.

ANIMAL   Animal or instinctual side of nature. By absorbing the energy of the animal symbol we integrate with a particular trait within our being, and can then draw on its strength.

ARCTIC ANIMAL   Frozen or undeveloped quality, symbolized by the animal.

BABY   New consciousness, new awareness. A refusal to care

for a baby means a refusal to bear responsibility for new wisdom.

BALL   Playing the game. Group consciousness.

BALLOON   Soaring, uplifting, releasing, moving beyond the physical.

BIRDS   Freedom, elevation, ability to move in more than one dimension. Messenger of the soul. A flock of birds is telepathy.

BIRTH   Birth to a higher self.

BOAT   Emotional body. Voyage through life.

BOOK   Akashic record.

BREAD   Communion, sacrament, sharing.

BREAST   Nourishment.

BUTTERFLY   Transformation. Metamorphosis. Reincarnation. Transition.

CAMERA   Standing outside of what is happening.

CAR   Physical body. Ability to move through life. Old car equals outmoded ideas.

CAT   Psychic protection, or attack – dependent on the dream. A kitten is immaturity, playfulness.

CAVE   Inner self.

CANDLE   Inner light, willpower.

CHAIR   Support.

CHILDREN   Joy, freedom, spontaneity. One's own inner child – sometimes abandoned child.

CIRCLE   Completion, wholeness, oneness with God.

CLOCK/WATCH   Time (too much? too little?)

COW   Domesticity.

CRAB   Defensiveness. Escape, vulnerability.

CRYSTAL   True self. Purity. Clarity. Divine light.

CUP   Emotional receptivity.

DANCE   Blending energy, movement, relaxation.

DEATH   Release, letting go, dying to the past or old habits. Need to release the quality inherent in a person who dies. Dreams of death can sometimes also prepare one for death – one's own or another's.

DESERT   Emotional aridity.

DEVIL   Fear.

DOG   Loyalty, faith. (Look at breed: mongrel, e.g., equals

mixed beliefs, poodle equals vanity and terrier equals inquisitiveness.)

DONKEY   Stubbornness; or the willingness to carry burdens.

DOVE   Holy Spirit.

DRUGS   Fantasy, illusion.

DUCK   Avoidance, e.g. to duck an issue.

EAGLE   Daring, courage, evolution.

EARTH   Firm foundation. If muddy, lack of foundation. Too dry equals lack of emotional nurturing. Grovelling in the earth is making a mess of life, abusing it.

EGG   Fertility, birth, new life.

ELEPHANT   Perseverance. Family.

FALLING   Humility, falling down on something.

FIRE   Purification. (Can sometimes predict illness.) Forest fire is a cleansing, balancing.

FISH   Spiritual truth, Christ consciousness. Eating fish is to partake of spiritual truths.

FLIES, FLEAS, INSECTS   Malice, psychic attack, negativity, parasitic people.

FLOWERS   Emotional expansion, spiritual grace, life. Wild flowers mean simplicity, purity. Cultivated flowers are emotional development.

FLYING   Ability to use higher levels of consciousness. Expansion.

FOG   Confusion.

FOOD   Sharing, communion, spiritual and physical nourishment.

GARDEN   Consciousness. A wild garden means work to do on oneself.

GATE   New opening.

GLASS   Protection, insulation. Broken glass means something finished, over.

GRASS   Peace, life, health and healing.

HAIR   Virility. A haircut means shedding old concepts.

HEDGE   Protection.

HORSE   Strength, progress. The energy to carry one through life.

HOTEL   Transition.

HOUSE   Physical body. If a house has many floors it symbolizes different bodies, i.e. mental, spiritual, emotional and physical, plus different levels of consciousness. The basement is the subconscious. The attic means the higher consciousness. The kitchen is work, sharing, needs which arc being met. A bedroom means rest and renewal. Sharing a bed means working together with the person in the bed. Sexuality means merging one's own qualities with those symbolized by the other person. A living room is communication and sharing. A bathroom is the need to eliminate, cleanse, or to be in the process of so doing.

HOVEL   Spiritual poverty, self-denial.

ICE   Frozen condition, the need to thaw one's emotions.

ICE CREAM   Indulgence.

ISLAND   Isolation, separation.

JEWELS   Cut jewels signify grace, spiritual power. Uncut jewels are qualities which are waiting to be developed (see my book *The Power of Gems and Crystals* for a more detailed interpretation). To touch a jewel is to be recharged with its quality.

JOURNEY   Voyage through life.

KEY   To be ready for the next step, the answer to a problem. A bunch of keys means opening many things at once.

KISS   Brotherhood, brotherly love. If sensual, it shows conscious or unconscious sexual feelings between the people kissing.

LADDER   Ascension.

LAMB   Sacrifice, vulnerability.

LILY   Resurrection, purity.

LION   Power, ego, mastery.

LOBSTER   Insulation, hypersensitivity. (Shellfish generally mean a perceived need to armour oneself.)

LOCK   Precaution, protection. A broken lock can mean a lack of responsibility.

MARRIAGE   Union with the higher, soul self.

MASK   Concealment. Ego-personality. A mask breaking or cracking can mean the opening up of the real self.

MENSTRUATION   Release.

MILK   Nourishment from Divine Mother, spiritual truth.

MIRROR   The need to face oneself.

MONEY   Energy, exchange of energy.

MONK   Renunciation.

MONKEY   Inquisitive, playful.

MOON   Emotions, dredging up emotions from the past.

MOTHER   Nurturing power of the feminine, *or* 'witch-mother', abuse, criticism.

MOTOR   Power to move through life, acceleration.

MOUNTAIN   Effort to develop. Climbing a mountain is a spiritual journey towards evolution.

MUSIC   Experience of music of the spheres, healing, initiation into the power of sound vibration, contact with angelic spheres.

NAKED   Revealing self, ideas, freedom.

NECKLACE   Spiritual powers.

NEEDLE   Mending one's ways.

NEWSPAPER   Publicity, notoriety.

NUMBERS

   1: Will, initiative, inspiration.

   2: Duality, caring, sharing, partnership.

   3: Communication, expression. Trinity, or threefold aspect of God as Mother, Father and Son, or will, wisdom and love.

   4: Master of self and laws of earth. Initiation, sacrifice, karma as signified by the Cross.

   5: Freedom, expansion, versatility, five-pointed star as symbol of the perfected man.

   6: Balance (especially in relationships), heaven and earth, giving, service, synthesis. Marriage, emotion and thought.

   7: The number of the mystic, seeker of truth. Someone who looks at life from a different perspective.

   8: Power. Macrocosm, microcosm.

   9: Authority. Mastery over the lessons of life, overcoming challenges. Development of the higher will.

   10: The completion 'I am whole' or one with God.

   11: A Master Number, meaning that it has added potential – as do 22, 33, 44 etc. Each has a double dose of the quality of its original number.

   12: Cosmic order, discipleship, blend of world and spirit.

OCTOPUS   Being drained by others sucking one's life force.
OIL   Oil from well equals worldly support. Anointing with oil means discipleship.
ORACLE   Divination. Prophecy.
OWL   Wisdom.
PAPAYA   Cleansing, balancing digestion.
PARROT   Gossip.
PARTY   Celebration, joy, recognition of soul partners. Or letting go to the lower senses.
PEACOCK   Vanity.
PEN   Creativity, communication, written word, expression.
PERFUME   Healing, blessing, angelic presence.
PHOENIX   Transformation, evolution, spiritual teacher.
PHOTO   Self-examination.
PIG   Greed. Sensuality.
PLAY   Reviewing what we have planned for ourselves – from past, present or future.
PLUMBING   Elimination (if in public, means freedom). Releasing and letting go. If one is trying to find a secret place in which to act, it implies something to conceal, a sense of shame.
POLICE   Angel guides or teachers, the will of God, grace, protective and/or warning. A sign of care and love.
PREGNANCY   Preparing for the birth of a new level of understanding.
PRESIDENT   Authority.
PRISON   Limitation, holding back.
PROSTITUTE   Giving away power, abandonment to physical senses.
QUEEN   Goddess within, power of the feminine.
QUEST   Spiritual journey, search for the Holy Grail, search for the soul.
RABBIT   Timidity.
RACE   Competition, challenge.
RADIO   Ability to 'tune in', telepathic communication.
RAINBOW   Sign of God and angelic protection. Celebration.
RAPE   Violation of space, invasion of privacy.
ROCK   Strength, stability. If blocking way ahead, may symbolize an inner block to progress.

ROD   Power, strength, will.

ROOF   Mental stability. If in need of repair, we must be still, calm and relaxed to mend it.

ROPE   The cord connecting us to the physical body, or our emotional connection with others. If we are tied by rope, it is limitation. If breaking free, it is expansion.

SAND   Futility (quicksand), lack of foundation.

SCALES   Balance.

SCHOOL   Learning. College and university symbolize the Halls of Wisdom and Learning – researching one's own records.

SEASONS

Spring: New beginnings.

Summer: Completion. Harvesting of seeds sown.

Autumn: Re-evaluation, letting go.

Winter: End of cycle. Bare trees.

SHARK   Predator.

SLEEPING PILLS (drugs)   Escape.

SNAIL   Slow progress

SNAKE   Wisdom, healing, kundalini energy. If coiled, vulnerability. If semi-coiled, head out-thrust, means ability to care for oneself. If elongated, stretched out, it means healing power, often unrecognized by the dreamer.

SNOW   Frozen conditions.

SPIDER   Being trapped by another's power.

STAGE   One's appearance before others on the stage of life. Initiation to new creativity.

STAIRS   Ability to explore higher and lower dimensions of life.

STAR   Evolution. Expansion. Balance of heaven and earth. Unfolding of personality. Often symbolizes feelings of isolation caused by 'following one's own star'.

STATION   Night travel, expansion, movement through dimensions.

SUN   Communion with God, Christ, life, spiritual energies.

SWAN   Spiritual evolution, balance.

SWORD/SCISSORS   Power of discrimination, ability to cut through.

TABLE   Communication, sharing.

TELEPHONE   Telepathy, telepathic communication.

TOWER   Foresight, overview.

TRAIN   Flight.

TRAVEL   Expansion.

TREES   Essence of who you are. Look at how firmly grounded and rooted they are. Bare branches imply a stripped feeling, heavily leafed branches an impression of abundance. Branches which reach out mean protection. The weeping willow means depression, and the pussy willow affection and tenderness. The pine tree, the most psychic of all, is evergreen, symbolizing everlasting life.

TUNNEL   Moving through karma.

UMBRELLA   If open, protection. If closed, unaware of protection.

UNCLE   Paternal guardian.

UNIFORM   Tradition, inflexibility.

VEGETABLES   Natural nourishment. (Look at the need for certain nutrients in your diet.)

VINE   Fruits of experience.

VOICE   Hearing a voice in a dream usually symbolizes the voice of the teacher.

WAITER/WAITRESS   Ability to serve.

WAND   Action, direction.

WATCH   Timing.

WATER   Spirit or emotions. If clear, means purity. If muddy, implies guilt, lack of clarity.

WHEEL   Karma, experience. Means chakras, the seven vital energy points of the body. Chakra means 'wheel' in Sanskrit.

WIND   Cleansing, blowing away the past.

WINDOW   Astral protection.

YAWN   Spiritual depletion, draining of energy.

ZOO   One's animal nature restrained.

Colours

Each colour is a manifestation of the vibratory rate of a particular colour ray. Each ray has certain characteristics, and therefore to see colours in a dream indicates an alignment with, or need to focus on, the vibratory power (or quality of energy) contained within the colours seen. Absence of colour usually denotes absence of life, emotion and vitality.

AMBER   Life force, sun.

BEIGE   Detachment, non-involvement, neutrality.

BLACK   Absence of colour and light. Indifference. Unknowing.

BLACK-PINK   Destructive.

BLUE   Wisdom, clarity, truth, peace.

BLUE, PALE   Passivity.

BLUE, TURQUOISE   Freedom of expression.

BROWN   Introverted, retreating, going inside oneself. Concealment of identity.

GREEN   Life, health, healing, balance.

GREY   Detachment, aloofness.

GOLD   Enlightenment. Colour of God.

INDIGO (midnight/navy blue)   Imagination, intuition. Third Eye initiation.

LAVENDER   Spirituality – sometimes connects to asthma or difficulty with breathing at birth.

ORANGE   Emotional assimilation, physical digestion, release.

PINK   Love.

PURPLE/VIOLET   Transformation, spiritual responsibility, inspiration, spiritual healing.

RED   Physical energy, action, expansion. Lowest rate of vibration.

SILVER   Cool, mystical, moon initiation.

WHITE   Perfection (white light of Christ), purity. Highest rate of vibration.

YELLOW   Mental power. Determination. Assessment and joy. Sun, freedom of inner child.

Appendix

DREAM GROUPS
AND WORKSHOPS

In this century we have learned to take dreams seriously. In America, both the Stanford School of Business and Harvard University have developed programmes which teach business-men and women how to use dreams to solve problems and develop creativity and initiative. Gale Delaney, an American dream psychologist, says that doing psychology without using dreams is like doing orthopaedics without an X-ray. Around the world there are dream clubs, groups, newsletters, magazines, research centres and workshops, through which dreamers can share their dream experiences

In the course of my own dream therapy, I have discovered that heart-attack patients who are encouraged to pay attention to their dreams get better much more easily and quickly than those who do not. Part of this is due to teaching them simple breathing and relaxation techniques. Pregnant women who use dream therapy as part of pre-natal exercises give birth far more painlessly (sixty-five percent, according to research with which I've been involved). Students who practise dream-work learn more quickly, assimilate information better, and in exams have far more extensive and instant recall of the subject matter.

Dream sharing gives dreams more importance and helps dream recall. To share a dream can also add to your own under-standing of it. Other people's comments can help shed light on it, but you also 'feel into' the dream in a different way when you speak it aloud. Sharing dreams with a husband, wife, lover or friend can lead to deeper understanding, better communication, insight into unresolved issues as well as greater love and harmony. And family dream sharing is a wonderful way to encourage children to value their dreams and express feelings that they might otherwise hide.

If you are setting up a group it is important to get the basics organized first:

1. Decide the meeting place. Obviously this depends to some extent on the size of the group. If you are fifty you may need to hire a hall, while if you are six you can meet in someone's house – in which case will it be the same house every week, or will you take turns to be host? Plan beforehand to avoid confusion.

2. Choose times to start and stop, and stick to them. Group work requires a commitment to the group as well as to the subject in hand, and if people trail in and out whenever they feel like it nothing worthwhile can develop.

3. Be careful about numbers – avoid having so many that each member cannot share his dream. It is usually impossible to let everyone express himself in one evening, so it is better to work intensively with two or three dreams each time you meet. Let each group member recount his dream in turn, and allow enough time for discussion and group work after each dream is related.

4. Define from the start how long the group will meet – once a week for eight or twelve weeks? Once a month for a year? You can always make new arrangements as these draw to a close, but to set limits helps to consolidate group energy. My own group work ranges from 'one-off' three-hour sessions to eight consecutive three-hour weekly sessions. My workshops vary from a full weekend to a whole week or month. In each case, whatever discoveries the participants need to make in

that time are made. This is nothing to do with me. To set a time limit is like issuing a command to our consciousness to respond, and it does.

5. Set an ideal for the group. What do you hope to get out of this meeting? What is your overall aim? This helps to bring the objectives into sharp focus, as well as clarifying to each person why he is there.

These details may sound trivial, but they help give group meetings a firm foundation.

Once you have got to that stage, there are many ways in which you can explore your dreams together. But one or two elements should remain constant:

1. At the start each member of the group should make a statement about himself and why he is there, what he hopes to gain from it and to add to it. This could range from 'I am Mary Jane from Manchester' via introducing yourself as your latest dream character, to spending five minutes sharing the key points in your life or telling your whole life story.

   In month-long workshops we often take an entire week listening to everybody's life stories. This clears them out of the tellers' systems, and reminds us that we all have basically the same story – the same griefs, hopes, fears and joys – as everyone else. These stories usually awaken incredible dreams in the listeners, too, so that the dream becomes the life story and the life story the dream, and light is shed on both.

2. It is important to create an atmosphere of trust, so that each member feels safe and knows that whatever is shared is kept within the group. Open and close each session with a brief attunement, such as by saying a prayer or affirmation, lighting a candle or holding hands.

After these essential preliminaries you can get down to the main purpose of the group and decide which approach or approaches to adopt:

1. If the group at first finds it hard to concentrate – perhaps the members feel self-conscious – get the dreamer to share his dream three times, and ask the listeners to note any variations in the telling before working with the third and final version. This helps everyone to participate as active rather than passive listeners.

   If there is time, this is an excellent way of getting down to the true nuts and bolts of a dream, and it is essential for exercise no. 2 on p. 159. This is the method in which you pick three key elements from a dream, say what they mean to you, write a sentence and bring it back to one word. It can be done as successfully with another person's dream as your own, providing you remember that the three items become yours and are no longer associated with the dream itself. Having worked through the exercise, each person should then share what he picked, the meanings, the sentence and the word. It is a good way of assessing people's emotional focus.

2. In group work, we all work with one another's dreams. Rather than interpret what you *think* it is saying to the dreamer, it is better to listen as if it were *your* dream, and to *feel* what it says to you about you. In other words, remove the dream from the dreamer and apply it to what is going on in your own life. When these insights are shared, they can give the dreamer an expanded understanding of his own dream.

3. When listening to people share, listen not only to their story but also to their words and tone of voice. Watch their body language, and notice how your own body and emotions react. This all helps us to understand what is going on in both their and our own psyche.

4. Include some stretching, breathing, Om chanting or chanting vowel sounds associated with specific colours, as it loosens

people up – not just physically, but mentally and imaginatively too, so that answers and images float in more easily.

5. I prefer to ask questions rather than to interpret a dream, in order that each person gets his own answers. This includes asking what first steps he can take to actualize the dream in the day.

6. Some groups will prefer to work together on each dream, others to pair off or to divide into threes and then regroup before the end to discuss what has come up. This works very well for guided re-entry into a dream, as well as for carrying the dream backwards or forwards – to guide the dreamer through his dream to the point where it started or stopped, and see what happens next. It is a good technique if you only have a fragment of dream with which to work.

7. Some groups may like to practise lucid dreaming. Imagine rolling or lifting out of your body, and flying to a person or a place you really want to see. The more you can involve desire and enjoyment – if you long to go to Athens or to play with dolphins in Florida – the more your astral dreambody, the body of emotion, will try to get you there. If you were planning a holiday to a place you particularly enjoyed, you would devote considerable time and attention to it. Put the same attention into planning a lucid dream, and you are more likely to have one. Remember that lucid dreaming is often a prelude to astral travel.

8. Dream incubation was popular with the members of a summer camp workshop I was involved in running in America. We set up a special dream tent and decorated it with objects that had significance to the dreamers at the time. These included personal possessions such as crystals, gems, teddy bears and blankets, as well as shells and stones picked up from the beach. We devised a mini-preparation ritual, based on the American Indian Vision Quest rites, and as a result

both individually and collectively had some amazing dreams – many of which changed the dreamers' direction in life.

Group dream incubation needs to focus on a particular question, idea, purpose, problem or person to set it in motion. At this time the group decided to ask for a dream to solve major problems that Lucy, one of its members, was having at work. Although no one person got the complete answer, the results were extraordinary. Tom dreamed of seeing Lucy in a morgue, while outside brilliantly coloured images of life passed by. Jenny saw a three-year-old child trying to climb out of a window into a garden, while behind her lay a heap of mechanical toys. Judy saw Lucy mowing grass and cutting hedges, while George saw a young boy fighting to get out of an over-filled bedroom. As each person contributed his dream, a picture of Lucy emerged as someone trapped in something that was not alive or real for her. When Jenny shared her dream, Lucy remembered wanting as a child to play outside, but she was never allowed to get dirty or untidy. She wanted to climb trees, throw stones and dam streams.

Six months later, Lucy became a gardener and felt thoroughly happy. Her problems disappeared.

9. You might want to complete a session, particularly a long one, by devoting some time to making Mandalas using key symbols, colours, animals and flowers from the dreams you have shared. A Mandala or Shield of Power, especially when made from a series of dreams rather than just one, lays before you the story of your own unfolding wisdom, and can become a source of great energy the more you study it. Because it brings together the conscious and unconscious, it stimulates the one to act upon the other.

FURTHER READING

Artemidorus *Oneicrocritica* (Original Books 1991)

Bach, Richard *Jonathan Livingstone Seagull* (new edn. Pan Books, 1973)

Bro, Harman H. (ed) *Edgar Cayce on Dreams* (new edn. Aquarian Press, 1989) and any other Edgar Cayce books

Colton, Ann Ree *Watch Your Dreams* (ARC Publishing, 1973)

Cott, Jonathan *The Search for Omm Sety* (Arrow, 1989)

Fortune, Dion *Applied Magic and Aspects of Occultism* (Aquarian Press, 1987)

Freud, Sigmund *The Interpretation of Dreams* (new edn. Penguin, 1991)

'Fynn' *Mister God, This is Anna* (Fountain Publishers, 1987)

Garfield, Patricia *Creative Dreaming* (Ballantine, 1985)

Haich, Elisabeth *Initiation* (Unwin, 1974)

Halifax, Joan *Shamanic Voices* (Dutton) & *Shaman: The Wounded Healer* (Thames and Hudson, 1982)

Hall, Calvin Springer *The Meaning of Dreams* (McGraw, 1966)

Harding, Esther *Woman's Mysteries* (new edn. Century, 1989)

Hobson, Allan *The Dreaming Brain* (Penguin, 1990)

Holbeche, Soozi *The Power of Gems and Crystals* (Piatkus, 1989)

Jung, Carl *Man and His Symbols* (new edn. Pan Books, 1978)

Inayat Khan, Hazrat *The Sufi Message* (East–West Publications)

Lubicz, Isha Schwaller de *A Practical Guide to the Mythical Teachings of Ancient Egypt* (Inner Traditions, 1989)

Markides, Kyriacos C. *The Magus of Strovolos* (new edn. Penguin, 1990)

Muldoon, Sylvan and Hereward Carrington *The Projection of the Astral Body* (new edn. Century, 1989)

Peck, M. Scott *The Road Less Travelled* (new edn. Arrow, 1990)

Plato *The Republic* (Penguin, 1970)

Roberts, Jane *The Coming of Seth* (Pocket Books, 1987) and any other Seth books

Spalding, Baird T. *Lives and Teachings of Masters of the Far East* (De Vorss)

USEFUL ADDRESSES

Fellowship of Inner Light
P O Box 23
Yateley
Camberley
Surrey GU17 7DW

Association for Research and
Enlightenment (ARE)
P O Box 595
Virginia Beach
VA 23451
USA

Ann Ree Colton Organisation
ARC Publishing
P O Box 1138
Glendale
California 91209
USA

Paul Solomon Foundation
620 14th Street
Virginia Beach
VA 23451
USA

Both ARE and the Paul Solomon Foundation have dream groups worldwide.

INDEX

Aboriginals 76–87, 94, 99, 101
Abydos, Sety temple at 118–19
active imagination 70–1, 161
African Xhosa tribe 77, 89–97, 101;
    becoming a medicine man 90–2; dream
    culture 92–6; listening to izibilini 96–7
Akashic record (Akasia) 22, 51, 149
Alpha rhythm 58, 150
altruistic astral travel 137
American Indians 74–5, 77, 97–101, 106,
    186; sun-dance of 33; Vision Quest 75,
    99–101, 186
ancestors, dreams as communication
    from 90–7
animals as dream totems 93
animus/anima 70, 124–5
archetypes (Jung's term) 69–70
ARE (Association of Research and
    Enlightenment) 21–2, 57
Aristotle 20, 59
Arnold-Forster, Mary 73, 144
art and dreams 154, 163–4
Artemidorus of Ephesus 65–6
Aserinsky, Eugene 60–1
Aserinsky, Armond 60
Asklepios 105–8
astral travel 137–8; and dreaming 137,
    141; and OBEs 140–1
auras, seeing 142
auto-suggestion 128
Aztecs 33

Babylonians 33, 36, 51
Bach, Richard 113–14
Beta rhythm 58
big and little dreams 119–20
birth and death 136
Black Elk 74–5
brain research 58–60
brainwave rhythms 58
breathing control 148
Breuer, Dr Joseph 64

cancer, dreams preparing for death by 24,
    25, 134
Castenada, Carlos 128, 141
Cayce, Edgar 20, 21–2, 53, 57, 58, 65,
    114, 153

change, dreams preparing for 24–5, 36–9
chanting before sleeping 149
childhood and dreams 40–9, 61, 124,
    126–7; Senoi 87–9
China, ancient 12. 34, 125
Christianity 92, 121
circle as symbol 68
collective subconscious (Cayce's term) 21–2
collective unconscious (Jung's term) 18, 21,
    27, 68–9
colours in dreams 181
compensation dreams 124–5
complex (aka 'hidden impulse': Jung's
    term) 67–8
confronting and conquering danger in
    dreams 87–8, 125, 160–1
consciousness, sleep as altered state of
    50–63
creativity: dreams stimulating 7–8, 87–9,
    129; to invoke dreams 154
Cross symbol 120–1
crystals: for invoking dreams 135–6, 147,
    150; for remembering dreams 147; for
    storing cares of the day 145;

dawn, as easiest time for dream recall 155
death: and astral travel 137–8; and
    birth 136; dreams of 130–7; dreams
    preparing for 24, 134–5; other forms of
    death dream 135–6
Delta rhythm 58
Deunov, Peter (aka Beinsa Douna) 34
dialogue, dream 156, 161–2
dreambody (Mindell's term for the
    unconscious) 76
dream pillows 146–7
Dreamtime (Aboriginal) 77–87, 94; mystery
    of 83–6

EEG (electroencephalogram) 60
Egyptians, ancient 8, 33, 35, 51, 65,
    111–12, 118–19, 129; rites of 102–3
empathy and telepathy through dreams
    54–6
Epidaurus 105, 106
Essenes 52–3
ethnic dreaming traditions 77–101
exploring your dreams 157–65

extracting three major points from dream *159–60*
extra-terrestrial intelligence *143*

feelings in dream, describing *157*
Fisher King legend *15–18, 40, 42*
five-pointed star (pentagram) *10*
free association *65, 68*
Freud, Sigmund *20–1, 58, 58, 64–5, 68, 74* and Jung *71–2* and the unconscious *66–7*
Fromm, Eric *73, 75*

Galen *59*
Gandhi, Mahatma *116*
Gates of Ivory and Horn *103*
Gestalt therapy *48, 74–5, 127*; applied to dream retelling *162–3*
gift, demanding/asking for (at end of dream: in Senoi culture) *88*
Giza pyramids *111–12*
global change *11–12*
Greeks, ancient *20, 33, 36, 51, 65, 102, 103–8, 109, 111, 129, 130*; and dream incubation *106–8*; and oracles *103–6*
groups and workshops *182–7*

Hall, Calvin *73–4*
hallucination and dream deprivation *61–2*
Harding, Esther *34*
He (Johnson) *104*
healing dreams *123*
health warning (prodomic) dreams *122*
Holy Grail, quest for *15, 17*
Hopi Indians *98, 101*
Humanistic and Transpersonal Psychology *73*
hypnagogic images *29, 58–9*
hypnosis *64*

ignoring your dreams, avoid *164–5*
Igqira (African witch doctor) *93–4, 95*
imagination, value of *18–20, 48*
Increase/Decrease prayer *110–11*
incubation, dreams *65, 102–12, 123, 186*; sexual *129*
Indian yogis *58*
initiations: major *120, 131–2*; minor *120*
inner dialogue *127*
inner stranger *130–4*
inner teacher-guides *132–4, 155*; *see also* spirit guides
inspirational writing *153*
instinctual astral travel *137*
intelligent soul (aka 'the source', 'higher self' etc) *26–7, 29*
interpretation of dreams, practical *165–71*
Inyanga (African medicine man) *90–1*
Ixhwele (African herbalist) *93–4*

James, William *8, 57–8, 132*
Jesus Christ *92, 120–1*
Johnson, Robert *104–5*
Johnson, Samuel *50–1*
journal writing *127, 145–6*
Jung, Carl Gustav *8, 16, 20, 21, 27, 31, 66, 67–72, 73, 76, 93, 104, 116, 121, 132, 134, 143, 161*; and active imagination *70–1*; and archetypes *69–70*; and collective unconscious *18, 21, 27, 68–9*; and dream symbolism *68*; and Freud *71–2*

karma *113*
Kleitman, Nathaniel *60–1*
knowledge, dreams as source of *111–12*
Krippener, Dr Stanley *61*
Krishnamurti, Jiddu *145*

light, returning to *47–8*
listening to your dreams *29, 153*
little and big dreams *119–20*
lost child, dreams revealing *40–9*
love, our need for *45–7*
lucid and pre-lucid dreams *127–9*

magnetic north, setting bedhead towards *147*
major initiation *120*
Mandalas *187*
Mantram before sleeping *149*
Maury, Alfred *59, 72*
meaning of dreams, applying to your life *158*
meditation: and OBEs and astral travel *140–1*; before sleeping *149*; to aid dream recall *155*
Meguid, Mahmud el *111–12*
message, dreams with a *36–9*
Mindell, Arnold *73, 76*
minor initiation *120*
moon: –energized water *147*; as feminine principle of God *33–4, 35–6*; Goddess (Astarte) *36*; power of *35–6*; worship of *34*
myths, dreams unlocking your inner *28*

near-death experiences (NDEs) *136–7, 138*
near-death trance *58*
neurosis, origins of *71–2*
nightmares, dealing with *25–6, 125–6, 165*
notes under pillow *56, 109*; asking for dream *149–50*

OBEs *see* out-of-body experiences
Oedipus complex *66, 67, 72*
Om, the *149*
oracles, Greek *103–8*
out-of-body experiences (OBEs) *138–41*

painting or drawing your dream *154*, *163–4*
Parsifal legend *15–17*
passive child abuse *42–3*
past lives *113–19*; encountering through dreams *116–18*; dream life of Omm Sety *118–19*; searching for clues and getting in touch *115–16*; value of past live therapy *114*
pentagram (five-pointed star) *10*
people in dreams, noting *158*
Perls, Fritz *73, 74–5, 162*
personality dream (little dream) *120*
Phambana (madness) *94*
Philemon (Jung's spirit guide) *134*
Plato *50, 57, 69, 105, 136*
Pluto, influence of *13–15*
positive outcome in dreams, obtaining *160–1*
practical dream interpretation *165–71*
precognition and prophesy through dreams *23–4, 26, 120–2*; and UFOs *142*
pre-lucid dreams *127*
prodomic (health warning) dreams *122*
psychosis and dream deprivation *61–2*

questions: to dream figures *125*; dreams answering *30, 109–11*; to inner teacher-guide *155*

Ramón y Cajal, Santiago *60*
realizing your dream *153–4*
receptivity for sleep *144–5*
recurring dreams *126–7*
re-entry, dream *160–1*
re-experiencing your dreams *155*
rereading your dreams *155–6*
reincarnation *113–19*
relationship with ourselves *43–4*
relaxation: and Alpha rhythms *58–9*; and astral travel and OBEs *140*; before sleeping *148–9*
REM (rapid eye movement) *60–3, 64*
remembering your dreams *151–7*
Research Society for Process Oriented Psychology *76*
risks, taking *12–13*
Romans *59, 63*

St Denis, Hervey *72–3*
Sangoma (African shaman) *90–1*
schizophrenia *68–9*
Schweizer, Robert *92–3, 95*
seeds, sorting *130–1*
Senoi culture (of Malaysia) *52, 61, 87–9, 99, 101, 125, 160–1*
Sety, Omm (née Bentreshyt; Dorothy Eady) *118–19*

Sety, Pharaoh *118–19*
sexual dreams *129*
shadow, the *70, 124–5*
sharing dreams *182–7*
sleep(ing): as altered state of consciousness *50–63*; different states of sleep *58–60*; phenomenon of *50–1*; pills inhibiting dreams *151*; preparation for *52–3, 144–51*; and REM *60–3*; as route to understanding others *54–6*; in same room as others *55*; as source of spiritual nourishment *51–2*
Socrates *133–4*
Solomon, Paul *19, 22, 26, 29*
soul dream (big dream) *120*
spirit guides, dreams as communication from *90–7*; *see also* inner teacher-guides
spiritual nourishment, sleep as source of *51–2*
Stevenson, Professor Ian *113*
Stewart, Kilton *87, 88*
summing up: day *145*; dream *158*
sun: as creative masculine principle of God *33*; – dance *33*; transforming power of *30–1*; as source of energy and intelligence *32–4*; Tree (Egyptian Hathor) *33*; worship of *34*
symbols, dream *68, 75, 153, 158, 165–70*; glossary of *173–81*
making use of 'signposts' *172–3*

telepathic dreams *124–5*
telepathy: and empty through dreams *54–6*; and UFOs *142*;
Theta rhythm *58*
Tibetan dream yoga *53*
titling your dreams *155–6, 157*
triggers for lucid dreaming *128, 150–1*

UFOs (unidentified flying objects) *141–3*
understanding others, sleep as route to *54–6*

Vision Quest *75, 99–101, 106*
visits from ancestors, dreams as *90–7*
visualization *123, 127, 152*; inducing deep sleep and profound dreams *150–1*; and OBEs and astral travel *140–1*

waking up slowly for dream recall *152*
Wei Chi *12–13, 27*
wild beast nature, dreams revealing our *57–8*
wisdom, dreams as route to *27*
women, power of Aboriginal *86–7*
writing down your dream *148, 152*; *see also* inspirational writing; journal writing; notes under pillow

Zulus *90–1*